P9-DXH-592

DATE DUE

MY 20 '97	NO 4 02		
	DE 13 03		
AP 29	DE 2 04		
DE 15 98			
AG 5 99			
DE 3 99			
AP 11 00			
OC 27 00			
NO 22 00			
FE 22 01			
NO 13 01			
DE 19 01			
AG 1 02			
NO 20 03			

Teaching Tolerance

Teaching Tolerance

RAISING OPEN-MINDED, EMPATHETIC CHILDREN

Sara Bullard

DOUBLEDAY

New York / London / Toronto

Sydney / Auckland

PUBLISHED BY DOUBLEDAY
a division of Bantam Doubleday Dell Publishing Group, Inc.
1540 Broadway, New York, New York 10036

DOUBLEDAY and the portrayal of an anchor with a dolphin are trademarks of
Doubleday, a division of Bantam Doubleday Dell Publishing Group, Inc.

Book design by Maria Carella

Library of Congress Cataloging-in-Publication Data
Bullard, Sara.
Teaching tolerance / Sara Bullard.—1st ed.
p.   cm.
Includes bibliographical references and index.
1. Prejudices in children.   2. Prejudices—Study and teaching.   3. Toleration.
4. Parenting.   I. Title.
BF723.P75B85   1996
649′.7—dc20   95-36045
CIP
ISBN: 0-385-47264-1

September 1996

1   3   5   7   9   10   8   6   4   2

First Edition

Information
for Educators

Teaching Tolerance, a project of the Southern Poverty Law Center in Montgomery, Alabama, was founded in 1991 to provide classroom teachers with resources for promoting harmony in the classroom. The twice-yearly magazine *Teaching Tolerance* and a series of video-and-text curriculum kits are available for use in school, church, and community education programs. For more information, write to:

Teaching Tolerance
400 Washington Ave.
Montgomery, AL 36104
Fax: 334/264-3121

Acknowledgments

My friends and colleagues at the Southern Poverty Law Center nurtured this work with their patience and wisdom. Special thanks to Morris Dees, for his courageous and creative example; to Danny Welch, for his early encouragement; to Eddie Ashworth and Jim Carnes, for their thoughtful readings; and to Elsie Williams, Paul Newman, Glenda Valentine, Sophia Seals, and Rodney Diaz, for continuing to make the Teaching Tolerance project a success. Thanks also to Haynes Owens and Renee Cummings for reading portions of this manuscript. I have been strengthened over the past few years by the friendships of Amy May, Joe Roy, and Richard Cohen—thank God for you. And, finally, my thanks to all the children, too numerous to name, who have made me laugh and made me think.

For my parents, Jack and Becky Bullard

Contents

CONTENTS

Foreword
by Alvin F. Poussaint

Thirty years after participation in the civil rights movement in Mississippi, I appreciate that teaching tolerance is still one of our most urgent yet challenging responsibilities. Intolerance is so intractable in some cultures and individuals that many wonder whether we will ever be successful in eliminating it. From a physician's perspective, the chronicity of prejudice is a danger to our health and well-being. Historically, it has had disastrous consequences: the persecution, enslavement, and murder of untold millions. "Ethnic cleansing" massacres and human rights abuses endure around the world—a harsh and sordid reality. Bigotry, whatever its origin, endangers human survival, and we must not pessimistically retreat in our fight against it.

The United States, often viewed as a model society with a democratic political system, struggles to foster tolerance and protect minority rights. Though far from finished with its work, the U.S. has had some success in mitigating ethnic conflict and discrimination. The Civil Rights Acts of 1964 and 1965 have been critical to the process. Legal discrimination was outlawed, voting rights guaranteed, and affirmative action programs (currently under threat of being dismantled) were established for minorities and women.

Although preventing legal discrimination is essential, *Teaching Tolerance* reminds us that laws alone are not enough to change personal biases. Intolerance and insensitivity need attention in our day-to-day interactions. De facto segregation and discrimination are still serious worries. The incidence of racial and ethnic attacks and assaults against women, gays, lesbians, and other disparaged groups remain high.

Victims, especially children, of even mild prejudice may suffer emotional damage that can significantly impede normal function. Sara Bullard forcefully details how offensive, hateful language and insensitivity can inflict psychological damage. Nevertheless, a backlash has surfaced to what many view as a submission to political correctness in speech and behavior. Some individuals are angrily resisting change; they want a "right" to their prejudice. In other instances, some contend that regulations against "hate speech" violate the Constitution's protection of free speech. Institutions are currently grappling with these issues.

However, *Teaching Tolerance* is not about being politically correct; it is about embracing respect for all people who have differences based on race, religion, gender, sexual orientation, disabilities, class, or other circumstances. Bullard argues that prejudice is not innate; it is primarily learned attitudes that originate in the home and environment.

Multicultural education, therefore, can help our children interact positively with different members of society. Teaching the next generations to be free of prejudice is a critical antidote to future victimizations. Teachers and parents must understand *Teaching Tolerance* in this context of *prevention*. Readers willing to undertake the challenge will find practical guidelines and step-by-step suggestions.

Most of us can benefit from education, but research indicates that highly prejudiced people are emotionally troubled and may need special help. Is bigotry then a manifestation of mental illness? Certainly, in its milder forms, it is not. However, if prejudice leads to physical attacks and murder, such regressive acting-out can be viewed, without stretching the imagination, as psychotic. Wouldn't we all agree that Nazis are deranged? Intolerant extremists are paranoid and project blame onto a scapegoat. They have negative delusions about members of targeted groups and their reality testing is impoverished. This pattern of symptoms easily supports the criteria for a mental ailment.

Unfortunately, such a categorization is not found in our psychiatric nomenclature. Individuals may suffer from "acute anxiety" and "acute depression," but there is no category for "acute bigotry" or "malignant prejudice."

In my opinion, if extreme intolerance is seen as a mental disorder, there can be some real benefits. First, it would suggest that those afflicted need treatment and could recover with help. Second, we would become committed to *preventing* the development of this deranged perspective. Of course, a diagnosis of "acute bigotry" would not excuse perpetrators from personal responsibility. Individuals must be held accountable and be encouraged to change.

Above all, we must acknowledge that intolerance is damaging to each and every one of us as well as to society. The author suggests, too, that the person you may help the most by embracing tolerance is yourself:

> The distrust and misunderstandings that characterize our racial frictions are symptoms of an intolerance that handicaps all our relationships: between mother and child, husband and wife, employer and employee, teacher and students, friends and relatives.

Teaching Tolerance is an excellent presentation of a program for the prevention of prejudice. We should take it to heart.

Alvin F. Poussaint, M.D.
Clinical Professor of Psychiatry
Harvard Medical School, Boston
1996

Foreword
by Morris Dees

Few are more qualified than Sara Bullard to suggest how parents should educate themselves and their children to be more tolerant, to accept others who are in some way different, and to live more harmoniously in our diverse community.

Sara's parents provided her first examples of tolerant living. Her father, a white Southern Baptist minister in the theological tradition of Dr. Martin Luther King, Jr., was among the first in the South to open his church doors to blacks. Jack Bullard went on to help spearhead peaceful school integration in Charlotte, North Carolina, where court-ordered busing plans threatened to disrupt a fragile racial peace in the aftermath of the Civil Rights Movement.

Sara first put her parents' ideals and examples in practice as a teenager, serving on a student human relations council at her newly integrated junior high school. She continued her interest in civil rights through her studies at the University of North Carolina and during her career as a journalist. She began working full time in the field of human rights in 1985, investigating white supremacist activity for the State of North Carolina and, later, for the Southern Poverty Law Center.

In 1991, Sara started Teaching Tolerance, the education project of the Southern Poverty Law Center. Five years later, *Teaching Tolerance* magazine is seen by half a million teachers, and the project's curriculum kits are being used in more than fifty thousand schools nationwide.

Sara is not a parent or an educator, but both parents and educators marvel at her insight. Aside from the many national awards won by Teaching Tolerance, the proof of its effectiveness is in the overwhelming gratitude of teachers who have found in this project both practical ideas for change and a renewed reason for hope.

In this book, Sara makes the complicated simple. Her theme is timeless: we are all intolerant. We must first look at ourselves. We should set good examples for our children and teach them tolerance.

Children follow examples, not hollow *do's* and *don'ts*. My father was a white Alabama cotton farmer who never challenged segregation or spoke out for civil rights in the 1950s. But when I saw him use the same dipper to drink water that had just been to the lips of a black field worker, I viewed the "white" and "black" water fountains in a different light. My parents treated blacks as equal human beings at a time when my playmates' parents treated them as second-class citizens.

A white father sitting on his porch with his young son teaches intolerance if he wonders aloud whether a black man coming down their street "was robbing a house." On the other hand, he could give his son a powerful message of caring and tolerance if he offers help or simply extends a friendly greeting. The same would be equally true for a black father and son in a different neighborhood.

Most of us are burdened with prejudice and intolerance from our families, friends, and, unfortunately, many of our leaders. There should be no shame in admitting we harbor some prejudice on issues such as race, religion, and sexual orientation. What is shameful is our failure to examine those prejudices. Before we can effectively help our children, we must deal with our own intolerance.

This book is a good place to begin. We cannot completely guard our children from peer pressure, thoughtless remarks from relatives, or prejudiced actions of others. We can conduct our lives as living lessons for tolerance. I predict that you will learn much more than you'll teach your child when you read this book. Your child will then learn from your lives. Future generations in your family, it is hoped, will tell stories of things you did toward others in a loving, caring way.

Morris Dees
Executive Chairman
The Southern Poverty Law Center
1996

Introduction

I'm not a parent, but through the years I have loved many children. One of them was a four-year-old named Keisha, the most volatile of all the four-year-olds I taught in day care during the 1970s. Easy to anger and slow to calm down, Keisha spent at least part of every day being rocked by me while she cried.

I was holding her hand outside a public library one day while we waited for a class of children from another school to enter the front doors. The children we were watching were all white; my class was all black. Keisha noticed the difference and told me, "I hate white people. My momma hates white people and my sister hates white people and I hate white people." She spoke matter-of-factly, without a trace of hatred. Then it dawned on her. "Teacher, are you white?" she asked.

"Yes, I am," I said. "Do you like me?"

"I love you!" she said, and grinned.

"I love you, too," I said.

For Keisha at four, it was not yet necessary to reconcile her love for me and her hatred of white people. In fact, her hatred was no real hatred but only an idea she parroted. The danger was that she was growing up in a home where real hatred lived, and in such homes no one is exempt from harm. The anger that had infused her family life was evident already in Keisha's daily attacks of frustration and belligerence. She would soon need a generalized target for her anger, and her family had offered her one.

I could only imagine the roots of her family's anger. I remember an incident from childhood that, for a brief time, lit the fires of righteous rage in my own heart. One night we were coming out of the church where my father was pastor and saw flames rise from the school across the street. A cross was burning atop one of the buildings, presumably set because our church—a rural, Southern Baptist congregation— had officially opened its doors to all races. I learned quickly about the Ku Klux Klan and was thrilled when one of the young church members took off on his motorcycle in search of the suspected cross-burners.

I, like the children I was with, was most interested in seeing the transgressors punished. My mother and father clearly did not share our delight. The urge for revenge, to them, was as brutal an emotion as the hatred that inspired the cross-burning. It's too easy, they somehow let us know, to respond to hate with hate. Life is more complicated than that.

Children learn what we live. Before she was even capable of hating, Keisha had learned whom she was supposed to hate—in the same way, most likely, that the Klansmen who burned the cross at our church knew whom *they* were supposed to hate.

I learned to resist the racial stereotypes of my native South because my mother and father actively resisted them. I learned whatever sense of empathy I have because they were empathic. But I also learned to be competitive and to aim for perfection, traits that do not go well with the humility and open-mindedness required for real tolerance.

The path of tolerance is not always fun, but it is, at times, comforting and liberating. Most of all, it teaches us that we are small parts of something far greater than ourselves, and that we have a responsibility to preserve and to pass on all that we've learned about living together in peace.

All of our children will, at some time in their lives, be victims of intolerance. They will be rejected by others for a reason that is unfair: because of their size, their age, their gender, their skin color, their language, their beliefs, their looks, or their abilities. They will be hurt, some of them many times over. And one of the things they will learn from the experience of rejection is how to reject others.

We know this because we've lived it. In our memories are seared the moments when we felt out of place, put down, pushed aside, ignored, or ridiculed—as well as the moments when we turned our backs on others.

We are intolerant not because we are ignorant or racist or ill, but because we are human. The distrust and misunderstandings that characterize our racial frictions are symptoms of an intolerance that handicaps all our relationships: between mother and child, husband and wife, employer and employee, teacher and student, friends and relatives.

For too long, we have looked to large-scale social reforms to mend the rifts between us, and they have not. By such measures we may arrange ourselves in closer proximity to each other, but we don't become people who care about each other. We have sought to reform our society, but we have failed to reform our hearts.

Eleanor Roosevelt asked the question: "Where, after all, do human rights begin? In small places, close to home—so close and so small that they cannot be seen on any maps of the world . . . Unless these rights have meaning there, they have little meaning anywhere."

This book is not about the intolerance in our society; it's about the intolerance in ourselves. I say "ourselves" and I write "we" on the well-founded assumption that we are all alike in these aspects; we all share the need for community and the habits of exclusion. It is the intolerance in *us* that makes up the intolerance of the world.

But there is also a path toward tolerance available to us all, a path we have known for all time and in all cultures, one that relies on shared human values and a commitment to personal change. If the children among us are to discover what tolerance is, they must see it in action.

This book is an invitation to a life of tolerance, for ourselves first, for our children, and for our communities. The first three chapters focus on the human-ness of intolerance. None of us is exempt from the habits of rejection—our minds are hard-wired for it, and every heartache hones our talents for it. The fourth chapter outlines the kind of work required if we are to alter our instincts for intolerance. The remaining chapters walk through children's particular needs for security, self-expression, and moral guidance that, if respectfully met, will free them to be comfortable with themselves and with all kinds of others.

Throughout the book, you will find encouragement for keeping private journals that will help you clarify your own history of tolerance and intolerance, as well as suggestions for activities that can be undertaken as a family. Further resources are given at the back of the book.

Becoming tolerant is all about learning new habits of thought, feeling, and behavior. It is a difficult and deeply personal process, one for which we need help. This book is offered not as a detailed prescription for change, but as a general guide to understanding who we are as human beings and who we may be as parents who want to give their children a better chance.

Sharing the Journey

*The whole world watches to see
whether the democratic ideal in human
relationships is viable.*
GORDON ALLPORT

We want for our children a world where kindness comes easily. But then someone pushes them down on the playground and says, "You can't play with us." Dad and Mom argue through dinnertime. On TV, people are beaten, shot, strangled, stabbed, poisoned, and raped. In school, it's no secret who's smart and who's dumb, who's popular and who's not, who's got money and who hasn't. In the neighborhood, it is understood that certain kinds of folk are not to be befriended.

Before we are old enough to know or care about racial

and cultural distinctions, we are capable of intolerance. Children who have not yet learned who society's most frequent victims are will pick their own. I had no interest in playing with dolls or dressing up, so I was labeled a "tomboy." My little brother, born brain-damaged, was called "retard." An auburn-haired friend of mine remembers hearing, "I'd rather be dead than red in the head." Indeed, anything that makes a child "different" is justification for slander: glasses, braces, thinness, fatness, tallness, shortness, poverty, or wealth.

By the time most children are big enough to ride a bicycle, they know who the outsiders are and they know what to call them: jerk, fatso, nerd, faggot, greaser, nigger, chink, honky, cripple, dyke. No one had to explain these things. It's one of the inevitable lessons of being alive in America.

How things came to be this way is no mystery. Each of us begins life with the assumption that we are the most important person on the planet. The same thing that makes babies so lovable—that boundless joy of being "me"—is what makes toddlers so famously selfish. Among every child's first words are "no!" and "mine!" Young children are shameless in their attempts to control other people, and when control fails, they resort comfortably to cruelty.

Among the universal tools of intolerance devised by children is the taunt "Nya nya na na na! Nya nya na na na!" It's the sound of cruelty, the accompaniment to misery, and, remarkably, children all over the world learn it.

Intolerance, from a child's teasing to the most belligerent racial hatred, is driven by a natural self-centeredness made up of the illusion that we are more valuable than others and the underlying fear that the world may not conform to our wishes. We are born, for some reason, with these built-in handicaps to human relationships. We learn, as we mature, how to pick socially acceptable targets for our incivility. Children who need someone to pick on are fairly indiscriminate in the victims they choose. Adults who need someone to put down will not choose just anyone, but will find someone who meets their definition of the social "outsider"—a racial or religious minority, someone who's mentally ill or homeless, a gay person. The challenge, as one kindergarten teacher discovered, is not to reform our attitudes toward the targets of our intolerance, but to overcome the instinct for intolerance to begin with.

In Vivian Paley's kindergarten class in Illinois, a small girl named Lisa is "determined to identify those she dislikes at any given moment," according to Mrs. Paley. Lisa's friends can quickly become her enemies, and her enemies friends, for what seem the most arbitrary reasons. One day, Lisa cruelly ridiculed her classmate Hiroko by saying she smelled bad. The next day, by coincidence, both Lisa and Hiroko came to school with colds and notes from their parents asking that they be kept inside during recess. Finding herself alone in the room with Hiroko, Lisa said, "Pretend we live in a castle, just you and me, Hiroko, in a beautiful castle of gold and diamonds."

Lisa's wild swings of friendship and rejection did not surprise Mrs. Paley, who was a teacher of five-year-olds for over thirty years. On the contrary, they confirmed what Mrs. Paley believed all along: "It is the *habit* of rejection that grows strong; the identity of those being excluded is not a major obstacle."

We often think of intolerance as a social phenomenon—the hatred, prejudice, and stereotypes held against whole groups of people. But intolerance is also an everyday habit. We have a hard time getting along, and it shows up in all the measures of our social well-being: Half of all marriages end in divorce. Five children a day die of abuse or neglect. Domestic violence is the leading cause of injury to women. Juvenile arrests for violent crimes increased by 50 percent between 1988 and 1992. One out of twelve suburban high school students believes it is OK to shoot someone "who did something to offend or insult you."

In the final years of the twentieth century, gays and lesbians are the most frequent victims of hate crimes. The number of active white supremacist organizations in this country exceeds 250. And the long legacy of hatred and discrimination against African Americans has resulted in a country where, even today, white people are born healthier and live longer, are more likely to complete college and have higher incomes, and are less likely to be crime victims than African Americans.

The hatred that emerges from the human heart hurts all of us. And for millions of children, our habits of intolerance have left permanent scars.

There is an experiment that has been used for more than half a century by social scientists studying children's racial attitudes; it was devised by the psychologists Kenneth and Mamie Clark in the 1940s. Researchers offer children a choice of white or black dolls to play with and ask them a series of questions about which doll they prefer. The answers are almost always the same: When four-year-olds are asked which doll is the "nicer" doll, both black and white children pick the white doll. We have had decades of school integration and affirmative action, yet black children are still choosing the white doll, an outcome that is no surprise to the countless African American parents who have heard their children say, "I'm tired of being brown," and "When can I be white?"

Something is clearly wrong when young children, as soon as they get a look at the world we've made, are disappointed with the color of their skin.

The Roots
of Intolerance

What is it about human beings that leads us to fear differences and define enemies when what we clearly want is peace? That is the question that drove the Harvard social psychologist Gordon Allport in 1954 to explore the roots of intolerance.

America was on the brink of a civil rights revolution when Allport published *The Nature of Prejudice*. Schools were still segregated; African Americans were routinely discriminated against in all areas of life; Congress and the courts were just beginning to dismantle the social structures of racism. What interested Allport most was not so much the outward forms of intolerance as the reasons that human beings became intolerant in the first place. After all, he wrote, "human nature seems, on the whole, to prefer the sight of kindness and friendliness to the sight of cruelty . . . Normal men everywhere . . . like to live in peace and friendship with their neighbors; they prefer to love and be loved than to hate and be hated."

Yet there is an "endless antagonism" between groups of people that persists despite remarkable advances in almost every other area of human life. Allport wrote: "Civilized men have gained notable mastery over energy, matter and inanimate nature generally, and are rapidly learning to control physical suffering and premature death. But, by contrast, we appear to be living in the Stone Age so far as our handling of human relationships is concerned."

In the decades since the publication of Allport's book, social scientists have conducted countless studies, polls, and experiments designed to seek out the causes of intolerance. The bulk of their research supports Allport's central idea: we are all born with the capacity for tolerance and intolerance, and whether we tend toward one or another depends largely on how we are treated in our families.

Children who are brought up without strong bonds of family love, consistent discipline, and models of moral behavior become adults who are fearful, insecure, distrustful, and self-centered—the very traits intolerance thrives upon.

Children who are sure of their parents' love, who have had consistent guidance in moral issues, and who have witnessed the principles of tolerance in action in their own families are likely to become open-minded and compassionate adults.

Allport concluded that what matters is not so much what parents *tell* their children, but how they *treat* them. Tolerance emerges where love is certain—in families rich or poor, liberal or conservative, educated or uneducated. Without love and acceptance, without self-confidence and hope, children are ill prepared to deal with differences.

The implications of his findings are profoundly important for the children of the twenty-first century, whose futures will depend on how well they are prepared to live amid great diversity. All the evidence suggests that children without love and guidance are children who cannot care for themselves or for others. Yet the current crises of drug abuse, teenage pregnancy, poverty, suicide, and random violence are clear enough evidence that many of our children are growing up lonely and afraid.

What our society becomes will depend on what our families are like. This is a fact we've known for thousands of years. In the words of the ancient I Ching: "The family is society in embryo . . . Within a small circle a basis of moral practice is created [that] is later widened to include human relationships in general." The notion was echoed by the social scientist James Q. Wilson in 1993: "We learn to cope with the people of the world because we learn to cope with the members of our family."

Clearly, our diverse democracy will grow into a companionable place only if we plant the seeds of peace in our own homes. All that is precious and fragile about our democracy isn't preserved for the generations through laws or politics; it's preserved through families.

Tolerance Is . . .

In healthy families, tolerance is not an abstract moral concept but a way of learning to live with our differences. To preserve the bonds between us, we overcome disappointments, rejection, and loss. We sacrifice for those who are weak or in need. We feel each other's pain. We forgive each other's offenses. We offer each other attention and respect even when we cannot agree.

The same skills that can bring us peace in families can bring us peace in our world. Surely these skills are necessary for the preservation of community and society; they're also good for ourselves. When we hold hatred, fear, resentment, or anger for others, we create pain for ourselves. When we have tolerance for ourselves and others, we have peace.

Predictably, the English language offers no single word that embraces the broad range of skills we need to live together peacefully. Dr. Martin Luther King, Jr., used the Greek term *agape* to describe a universal love that "discovers the neighbor in every man it meets."

The various disciplines concerned with human behavior have also offered a variety of adjectives: "pro-social," "democratic," "affiliative." The word "tolerant," while it may irritate those who define it negatively, is in its positive sense the most appropriate.

These are the characteristics of tolerance as we use it:

- Tolerance is more than the ability to endure what we dislike. It is the ability to care for and feel connected to the great variety of human characters, even those people whose opinions or behavior we despise.
- Tolerance is not a product of politics, religion, or culture. Liberals and conservatives, evangelicals and atheists, whites, Latinos, Asians, and blacks—all people on earth—are equally capable of tolerance and intolerance.
- Tolerance is not an intellectual position. Being "for" tolerance does not make us tolerant, any more than being "for" humor makes us laugh. Tolerance has much less to do with our opinions than with what we feel and how we live.
- Tolerance is not something we can be talked into or out of. We teach tolerance in the same way that we become tolerant: by practicing tolerance.
- Tolerance is not moral relativity. It does not require us to value all opinions and behavior equally. Rather, it provides us with a context for making moral judgments that preserve the value of all people.
- Likewise, tolerance is not indifference. It does not give us the right to ignore violations of our deepest moral principles. It does allow us to reject the offense without rejecting the offender.

In general, tolerance is a way of thinking, feeling, and acting that gives us peace in our individuality, respect for those unlike us, the wisdom to discern humane values, and the courage to act upon them.

From Intolerance to Tolerance

To teach children tolerance, it's not enough to know what tolerance is. Parents must live it.

Children learn by watching their parents—it's the nature of our species. We teach our children most easily the things we have mastered ourselves. If table manners and safety skills come naturally to us, we don't have to ponder the best method of teaching them to our children. We simply guide our children through the motions that we already know by heart.

Yet many things we intend to teach our children are those we are still learning ourselves. And what we expect of them, we can't ourselves fulfill. This is particularly true in the realm of values. Justice, fairness, compassion, respect, empathy, forgiveness—we have an idea how they are manifested, but we are forever struggling to enact them. How can we expect from our children what we ourselves cannot give? Sharing toys, for instance, is one of the tougher challenges of childhood, and no wonder. How often are we willing to entrust our most prized possessions to the hands of another?

To give children a sense of values does not, fortunately, require parents to live perfectly by those values. It does require us to be firmly convinced of their importance in everyday life, to be able to articulate them with sensitivity and sincerity, to be aware when we violate them, and to share with our children our efforts, past and present, to incorporate those values into our own lives.

The journey toward tolerance begins when we recognize and try to heal the intolerance in ourselves. This is what Myrlie Evers-Williams, the widow of the slain civil rights leader Medgar Evers, learned in the years after her husband's assassination. She had every reason to become intolerant. She had endured years of segregation, humiliation, and death threats. Then, in 1963, she watched her husband die at the hands of a white supremacist. "I became consumed by hatred," she said. "The sound of 'Dixie' being played raised all kinds of feelings of hatred. Seeing the Confederate flag brought on pounding headaches."

Myrlie believed that it was right to have respect and compassion for all people, and that's what she wanted her children to learn. But in her heart she couldn't feel it, and there seemed nothing she could do about it. She simply hated white people.

Her sons and daughter would listen quietly as she cursed the white race, but they gave her looks that pointedly suggested, "You're not supposed to feel like that." And Myrlie felt the truth of something Medgar had told her years before: "If you hate someone, you are the one who ends up suffering."

Hoping to escape her pain, Myrlie Evers-Williams moved her family from Mississippi to a suburban California home. There, in a neighborhood full of white people, her hatred continued. She sat proudly among the white people at PTA meetings, sang hymns beside them in church, and waited in a quiet rage for the first opportunity to unleash her anger. It didn't come. She found, to her surprise, that she was accepted by, and actually had quite a bit in common with, her white neighbors.

The turning point came as she watched her children play day after day with their white friends. She realized simply that they were happy and she was not. "My hatred was destroying me. I couldn't continue my life like that."

In learning to accept others, she was able to accept herself. "I gradually came to the point where I did not look at another person and see their color first. And when I reached that level it was one of the most liberating feelings that I have had. It's absolutely amazing to me. People are people, and that's that. We have good and not so good in every ethnic group."

After the struggle for civil rights in society, the struggle for tolerance in her own soul was Mrs. Evers-Williams's greatest gift to her children. She had discovered that freedom was not possible as long as she was trapped in the internal prison of hatred and intolerance. In the end, no justification, no comparisons, could make intolerance anything but a miserable way to live. Once she recognized it in herself, she had to seek a way out.

A Beginning

Change begins when we look at ourselves in the mirror and tell the truth about what we see. If our goal is to guide our children toward lives of tolerance, we must first recognize the intolerance that shapes our own lives.

The next two chapters of this book describe the predisposition to intolerance and suggest the kinds of personal handicaps that make some people more likely to become intolerant than others.

The journey toward tolerance will take us into unfamiliar territory. It will require us to acknowledge an intolerance that we did not think ourselves capable of, and it will challenge us to practice tolerance in ways that we do not welcome. But the rewards of the journey are great. By learning to live peacefully together, we will help build a better world for all of our children.

﹌

WRITE IT DOWN

Reading these pages is only a first step, and by itself is not enough. Your task is to translate the general ideas put forth here into the particular circumstances of your past and your family's present. To help you do that, we give prompters for your journal at the end of each chapter.

There are good reasons for keeping a journal of your

voyage toward tolerance. Self-reflection is the first step toward self-acceptance, the first step toward tolerance, and a most valuable tool for parenting. When we make concrete our thoughts, feelings, and experiences by putting them on paper, we are forced to face ourselves. If we are honest about ourselves on paper, our fears lose their power, our resentments lose their sting, and we become open to hope and ready for change. In understanding ourselves, we become more understanding of others (including our children), and we are better able to give our children the tools for living peacefully in a complex world.

You are encouraged to write freely about your memories, thoughts, questions, and feelings as you read, and to reflect on the questions posed at the end of each chapter. You can also use these journal prompters to build bridges of understanding among your family members. Invite older children to keep their own private journals; share your feelings about some of your responses with one another; and use these questions to stimulate further family discussions.

↜

JOURNAL NOTES
CHAPTER 1

1. Why did you pick up this book?

2. What has already happened in your life or in your children's lives that makes tolerance a worthwhile topic to think about?

3. When you were growing up, how did members of your family demonstrate tolerance toward one another? How did they demonstrate intolerance? Describe specific incidents of both.

4. Make a list of personality characteristics (for instance, curiosity, compassion, caution) that you would like your children to have in their relationships with others.

5. Take another look at your answer to question Number 4. Identify the traits that seem compatible with tolerance. Are these also the traits you would like to possess? Which of these characteristics do you see in yourself? Which don't seem to fit?

CHAPTER 2

Mistaken Minds

*In the everyday world, one is under
the strongest compulsion to construe
things one way or another.*
WALKER PERCY

All human beings come equipped with brains that help us
process information quickly and efficiently. None of us is
exempt from the basic mental habits that make intolerance
common among us. Among these habits are our tendencies:

- to categorize new information;
- to generalize, to draw conclusions from limited evidence;
- to prefer the familiar over the unfamiliar;

· to rank ourselves and those around us;
· to seek conformity within our social groups.

We use these mental tricks so often that we are usually unconscious of them. They help us make sense of the world, and they help us feel secure. But if left unchecked, they can also lead to prejudice, stereotyping, and discrimination.

Categories

We simplify our world by categorizing—concluding that one person or situation is like another that we already know about. It's as if we have mental file folders; whenever we come across something new, we have a ready-made compartment in which to toss it.

The instinct to categorize, wrote Gordon Allport, is "the commonest trick of the human mind," and it's an essential skill of being human. Without it, we could not get through an ordinary day or follow our own train of thought.

But we can also use categorization to deceive ourselves. Faced with ambiguous evidence, we find it easy to make sweeping judgments based on what we already know, what we need, or what we desire—even when those judgments are mistaken. We use categorization when we fall in love, imagining a companion who can do no wrong. We use it when we go to war, defining an evil opponent. Toddlers use it to separate carrots and peas (things to eat) from beads and marbles (things to play with).

In the invented stories of kindergartners, there are wicked sisters and beautiful princesses, turtle heroes and sewer monsters—the bad guys are really bad and the good guys are terrific. There is little room for ambiguity. Dress-up clothes and doll houses are "things girls play with"; dominoes and trucks are "things boys play with."

This is how stereotyping begins. And on it goes through the years, until we seem to have a ready category for every new person we meet. Among the files we may keep handy are:

Category 1: *people who get on my nerves* (for instance, TV evangelists, pushy car dealers, people who stand too close).

Category 2: *people I will go out of my way to avoid* (say, the homeless, the handicapped, the mentally ill).

Category 3: *people who intimidate me* (police officers, gorgeous people).

Generalities

In the art of jumping to conclusions, we are all Michael Jordans. In childhood especially, we are eager to master our surroundings. We seek the comfort of having all the necessary information and being able to predict what will happen next. Children draw conclusions based on previous experience, not understanding just how limited that experience is.

A four-year-old child who had seen Chinese people only in restaurants concluded that *all* Chinese people ate in restaurants. Patricia Ramsey, the educational psychologist who described the child's logic, said the best adult reasoning could not convince this particular girl that Chinese people sometimes ate at home. She was not intentionally stereotyping; her mind was working normally for a four-year-old.

Such reasoning is common among the very young, Ramsey wrote in *Teaching and Learning in a Diverse World*. Small white children, for instance, often conclude that people with dark skin are dirty. It makes sense to them; after all, their own hands become dark when they get dirty and turn light again after they're washed. Only after personal observation do they accept that some people have naturally dark skin.

Innocent though it may be, a white child's judgment that a black child's skin is dirty can have harmful consequences. The child who is called "dirty" is confused and deeply hurt. The child's older brother, having experienced real prejudice, hears the same comment and assumes that the white child, like so many others, doesn't like black people. So into the file "racist" he puts the white child who knew no better.

Children must be excused their faulty reasoning. They try the best they can. There comes a time, though, when we are old enough to know better, and our generalizations may have more questionable motives.

A white woman raised in the early years of school integration prides herself on being open-minded. Yet when driving through a lower-income black neighborhood with her children, she hits the automatic door locks on her car. It's a sensible precaution, she tells herself. She knows someone who was robbed by an African American crack addict. Most of the arrests she sees on the news are of black men. The sound of the doors locking alerts her children to her fear. Even the youngest will get the message. In a single twist of reason, a mother has stereotyped all black people and, without saying a word, is teaching her children to do the same.

Familiarity

From birth until death, we make a vigorous attempt to fit all that's strange and new and surprising into what we already know—even when our views are mistaken.

When Copernicus suggested that the Earth circles the sun, no one believed him—not because his ideas were irrational, but simply because they contradicted the conventional wisdom that Earth was the center of the universe. The more sense Copernicus made, the more fearful people became, because their place in the cosmos was being questioned. They not only rejected the discovery; they persecuted the man who made it.

We use the same tactics today. We hold fast to old ideas and old attitudes because they make us feel secure. For the same reasons, we prefer people who are familiar to us—those who speak the same language, who dress the way we do, whose skin color is like ours.

The first thing we do when we encounter strangers is to notice the ways they are like us or different from us. And we gravitate toward those who are like us. This doesn't require a conscious effort; it comes naturally. Given a choice of seats on a crowded bus, we will pick the seat next to the person who seems most like us. Among the parents at the park, we introduce ourselves to the ones who look as if they could be members of our own families.

We are apparently born with a tendency to prefer the familiar and withdraw from the unfamiliar. In the second year of life, almost all children cry when left alone with a stranger. As their world enlarges, that fear lessens, but they generally remain wary of the strange. A toddler who meets a youth bent by cerebral palsy or a veiled Muslim woman might draw back in confusion, just as she would on seeing a hockey player in full uniform. Visible differences are short-hand for "them" until proven otherwise.

Decades after the end of legalized segregation, we adults still choose, by and large, to live in neighborhoods and attend churches that are racially homogeneous. At work, we may have superficial relationships with people of other cultures, but whom do we bring home for dinner? Which of our children's school friends do we invite over to play?

Finding a Place

The more insecure we are, the more desperately we need to define our place and the greater our fears of the world.

Many thinkers have wondered why this is so. One pessimistic conclusion, drawn by the writer Arthur Koestler, is that humanity is the victim of an evolutionary blunder, a mistake of brain development that makes us naturally unreasonable. Though Koestler's view never took hold, his evidence for human irrationality is disturbing. He described our ancient religious antagonisms this way: "For nearly two thousand years, millions of otherwise intelligent people were convinced that the vast majority of mankind who did not share their particular creed or did not perform their rites were consumed by flames throughout eternity by order of a loving god."

It's only moderately comforting to remember that humans are not alone in their fear of differences. We inherited this trait from our oldest ancestors, the apes. Chimpanzees are famously friendly among their own groups, but they "simply can't stand the sight of strangers," observed Carl Sagan in his book *Shadows of Forgotten Ancestors,* co-authored with Ann Druyan. Unfamiliar chimps provoke immediate outrage. They are routinely attacked and killed.

Even within a single group, the chimp who differs from the norm is shunned. In 1966, Jane Goodall was watching when a polio epidemic struck a group of chimps at the Gombe Reservation in Tanzania, leaving several chimps partially paralyzed. Goodall wrote: "Crippled by their disease, they were forced to move in odd ways, dragging limbs. Other chimps were at first afraid; then they threatened the afflicted, and then attacked them."

The insistence on the dominance of "our" group and the antagonism toward strangers is very common among animals. It helps ensure protection for the group's young and unity against outside threats. There is nothing like a shared enemy to strengthen the bonds of loyalty; recall how Americans postponed their differences to fight the Gulf War.

As the acceptable definition of our enemies changes, we redraw the boundaries between "us" and "them." We consider it rude today to disdain people for their physical disabilities, for instance, but we are quick to rebuke one another's differences in life styles or opinions. Consider the abortion debate, where opponents have characterized each other not just as mistaken, but as evil.

Inevitably, our search for sameness heightens our differences. Our group identities, though they may offer security, also isolate us. The more emphasis we place on our differences, the more we become alienated from the rest of humanity, and the more compelled we are to rely on our group status.

Ranking

Seeking a secure place most often means seeking a superior place. A chief tactic for finding comfort in a threatening world is to compare ourselves with others and then decide, by whatever act of imagination is required, that we are somehow smarter, stronger, kinder, or happier.

"The easiest idea to sell anyone is that he is better than someone else," Gordon Allport wrote. Everything about our competitive society encourages this, and it would be a rare person indeed who does not feel the urge to rank herself high among the company of humans.

The tendency begins, of course, in childhood. In the doll corner, there is a contest over who gets to be the mother. The role rotates between a couple of girls, and the rest defer to their rule. One girl never gets to be the mother. In the ordinary imaginative play of kindergartners, there can be just one mother, one hero, one boss; the rest scramble for position. Nearly always, someone is left out.

Children of different ages vary in their response to the outsiders among them. At four, they may show some sympathy. But by eight, they have learned how to enforce their perceived superiority with taunts, insults, and attacks. In every culture, kids are cruel.

We can use our tendencies toward ranking and generalization to imagine not just one person, but a whole class of people to be "less" than us. All we need is a clear way of distinguishing ourselves. For much of our history, white Americans chose as the demarcation line the most visible manifestation of human difference: skin color.

The history of segregation is a familiar one. Less familiar, but just as disturbing, are the attempts by scientists to rationalize white superiority. Researchers set to work many years ago to prove the biological supremacy of white people, primarily by measuring brain size and comparing head shapes. It was hard work and required a great deal of imagination, for in fact there is no gene that determines race, much less distinguishes one race as superior to another. Nevertheless, several of the best minds of science and some of our most honored leaders became convinced that Africans, Indians, and Asians were genetically inferior to whites.

Historians of science, notably Stephen Jay Gould, have since found that all of the so-called evidence pointing to white superiority was, conscious or unconscious, pure fabrication. Genetically speaking, we humans are just about the same everywhere.

What's fascinating about our capacity to deceive ourselves is the extremes to which we'll go. So genetics failed us; we'll find other ways to create human hierarchies. Education, looks, income, neighborhood, talent, careers, ideologies—we use them all as measures of our relative standing. And our motivation, though we ignore it, is transparent. For what reason would we rank our neighbors except to feel superior ourselves?

Conformity

The ability to conform is, like the other tendencies described here, a natural and necessary skill. We humans (unlike some animals that are born knowing how to get on with their lives) learn almost everything we need to know by watching and imitating those around us. To walk, talk, and eat, we have to copy how our families walk, talk, and eat. To earn praise, comfort, and love, we must act in an expected way.

A toddler's earnest imitation, a six-year-old's persistent questioning, and a teenager's obsession with hair styles and brand names all spring from the same drive to conform. We design our self-image according to the important people around us, for they are the ones we want to belong to. And if being accepted means ignoring our own values, we are willing to do that, too.

My friend Rick cannot forget the pre-adolescent excitement of group disobedience that led him to help vandalize the home of an elderly black man he adored. Now, years later, he acknowledges that he could have said "Count me out" and his friends would not have deserted him. At eleven, though, he went along with the plan, knowing even then that it would bring him shame along with acceptance.

An African American teenager gave up her best friend from childhood, a white girl, when her racial loyalty came under suspicion. Her black friends talked behind her back, asked her pointed questions, and avoided her whenever the white friend came around. She left her friend behind, and her regrets were lasting. She would have liked to have close friends of both races, but at that time and in that place it did not seem possible.

Peer pressure doesn't end in high school. Adults use religious, political, and intellectual gauges as justification for making judgments about their peers' worth. It is easy for us to look down on those who vote differently, for instance, and pretend that our bigotry is justified by the strength of our convictions. (We forget that our convictions allow us to reject opinions only, not the people who hold them.)

I was shooting pool with an Asian American woman. She was small, friendly, and was used to being condescendingly complimented on her good English (which was the only language she knew). While we were talking about a movie we had seen, two neatly dressed young men introduced themselves and joined us for a game of partners. We were halfway into a game of eight ball when they asked us to attend church with them. They were polite, not at all pushy. We declined with chilled civility and rolled our eyes after they walked away. One of us muttered, "Jesus freaks."

Why did we, who were sensitive to the distress of stereotyping, belittle them? My friend and I were apparently engaged in the old habit of reinforcing our own kinship by excluding another. It's one of those acts we disparage when we see it done by children, boldly and without disguise ("You can't play with us because she's my best friend and we don't like you!"). As adults, we're more subtle. We shore up the loyalty of our lunch cliques with gossip about the company management. We describe in the bylaws of our country clubs the traits of folk we won't consider for membership. And conformity quickly becomes exclusion.

Control

Tolerance is the ability to let people be who they are. It sounds simple, but we expect the world to operate as we want it to, people to act as we want them to act, and ourselves to become the people we imagine we are.

Our first act of tolerance must be to admit that people fall short of our expectations. We fall short of our dreams. Accepting the ambiguities of our nature and the disorder of our world without resentment or fear is one of the challenges of tolerance. The skills we're born with and acquire work together in complex ways to paint a picture of our world. But that picture can easily become an illusion, the story a myth, protected at great cost to human understanding.

To feel safe and to make sense of things, we often push our thought processes to the point of self-deception. Vivian Gornick, in her essay "To Begin With" (from the anthology *Visions of America)*, wrote that everything in her childhood reinforced her need to belong to the world and to understand it. From a devoted extended family, she learned very early who in the world was right and who was wrong and, by extension, the limits of who she could be.

She described growing up in the Bronx in the mid-1940s. "Us" were socialists, the "politically enlightened." "Them" were "the politically unenlightened . . . moral slugs." As Stalin exercised his power in the Soviet Union, Gornick found herself questioning what her family accepted as the unquestionable logic of socialism. It was a confusing and frightening doubt. In a family whose internal security was built on a single political theory, the ambiguities of reality had to be ignored lest the whole world cave in. But Vivian saw the injustices of the Soviet regime, and she couldn't fit them into what she knew about socialism. "Discrepancies in behavior nagged at me; questions arose for which there were no longer ready answers."

Finally, in 1956, at a kitchen-table argument with her aunt, she screamed, "Lies and treachery and murder!" And her aunt responded, "Lousy little Red-baiter!" And Vivian Gornick became an outsider in her own family. She wrote that later "the 'us' and 'them' of my life would become Jews and Gentiles, and still later men and women." But there always had to be an "us" and there always had to be a "them."

Surrendering to Mystery

Usually, it is only through the greatest effort in the most desperate circumstances that we come to redefine ourselves or the others around us. Tolerance is, in part, the courage to revise the stories we tell ourselves, the willingness to give up the security of neat misinformation for the surprises of reality.

Through mistakes of presumption, we deprive ourselves of life's wonder. An unshaven man who smelled of fish and liquor placed his tackle box uncomfortably close to the spot I was occupying on a South Florida pier one afternoon. Taking note of his appearance, I didn't speak. He asked about the fishing, and I answered shortly, without looking at him. I was about to move away from him to another spot when he began to recite Portia's speech from *The Merchant of Venice*: "The quality of mercy is not strained. It droppeth as the gentle rain from heaven . . ." I looked up in astonishment. He was watching the sea, casting his line and smiling. Our conversation lasted two hours.

People are so surprising, and the surprises are what make them interesting. But we so desperately need solid grounding in this turbulent world that we recoil from the unusual. Tolerance risks comfort for wonder, until we can surrender to mystery and another kind of comfort.

My uncles used to sing the old gospel hymn in perfect barbershop harmony:

> Farther along we'll know all about it,
> Farther along we'll understand why.
> Cheer up, my brothers, live in the sunshine,
> We'll understand it all by and by . . .

They let the last word linger on the sweetest chord, gently fading to a perfect, almost-whispered finish. And then they would break into soft laughter at the fantastical promise of the song. It was an inside joke that all the world could share: we'll understand it all by and by . . .

The truth is, no matter how neatly we picture our lives, no matter with what assurance we plan our futures, we are constantly being taken aback. Acknowledging that things are not what we expected and readjusting our visions to accommodate new clues are the chief characteristics of tolerance.

Being tolerant means being willing to think in new ways: to withhold judgment instead of leaping to conclusions, to change our minds to accept new information, to admit when we've made a mistake, to live with uncertainty and ambiguity. To do these things requires enormous courage, honesty, and, above all, a sense of personal security—emotional resources that in many of us are frail at best.

〜

JOURNAL NOTES
CHAPTER 2

1. Categories. We all categorize people, an activity Gordon Allport called the "commonest trick of the human mind."

List the *kinds* of people (not specific people) you would put into these categories:

1. People who get on my nerves.
2. People I will go out of my way to avoid.
3. People who intimidate me.

Now look at those you've listed. Pick a few, and write down all of the characteristics that you normally attribute to each kind of person. For instance, "police officers: white, bigoted, arrogant, stupid, uptight."

Your descriptions are stereotypes. To what degree are your responses to these people based on your prejudices?

2. Jumping to conclusions. Recall a negative experience with someone of another color. Describe it and name the feelings you had at that time. Did those feelings lead you to react differently at other times toward people of that color? Did you draw conclusions about that race based on your experience?

3. Sameness. You walk into a crowded waiting room at the doctor's office. There are two seats available, one next to an elderly white woman and one next to a young black man. There is someone coming in the door behind you, and you have to choose a seat quickly. Which one do you take? Why?

4. Ranking. You have a bumper sticker that reads: "My child is an honor student." Driving your child to school one day, you see another bumper sticker: "My child can beat up your honor student." For what reasons do you think that parent chose such a slogan? Why did you choose yours? What messages do the bumper stickers send about your children? About yourself?

5. Conforming. Recall a time when you were talking with someone who made derogatory comments about a person or group of people. He or she assumed that you agreed with the opinion, but you don't. How do you feel? How do you react? Why?

Recall a time when you overlooked your own values so as not to offend someone. Describe the incident, name your feelings, and suggest to yourself one way you might have responded differently.

6. Surprises. Describe one time when you were wrong in your judgment of another person. What did you base your initial judgment on? What led you to see that you were mistaken? How did you feel?

Pain
and Prejudice

*Ultimately, whoever hates, hates his
brother.
And when he hates his brother,
he hates himself.*
ELIE WIESEL

In our best dreams and the rarest of waking moments, we
are at home in the world and at peace with ourselves. We
imagine we had that feeling once, the contentment of a
child, limp and nodding on the edge of sleep, in the safety of
her mother's arms, all worries and fears forgotten. And
though most of the time such a feeling is unreachable if not
unthinkable, we can't help sensing in the pressures of ordinary life that some kind of peace is missing.

So we spend our lives trying to get comfortable,

squirming and fretting and trying to wiggle our way into that safe place.

In a town where I lived, there was an overweight girl who rarely smiled, was frequently sick and quick to anger, and moved with the awkward shyness of the self-conscious. She was a middle child. Her older brother was handsome and athletic, and her younger sister was bright and gregarious. Maggie was the outcast. Her mother told her she was fat. Her brother told her she was stupid. Her father ignored her. The neighborhood kids pushed, teased, and hit her. She was the one left hiding when they abandoned a game of hide-and-seek to ride their bikes down the street.

The more abuse she suffered, the more unpleasant Maggie became. If children were splitting a candy bar, she demanded more than her share and cried if she didn't get it. If she lost at a game, she screamed that the others had cheated and ran off to tell her mother. She'd push kids off the jungle gym and laugh if they cried. And she told lies— wild, ridiculous stories about the prizes she'd won, the important people she knew, the tricks she could do.

At nine, Maggie was filled with the need for love and the compulsion to hate. She would scream at her brother, sister, and mother, "I hate you! I hate you! I hate you!" But her cruelest arrogance was reserved for a disabled boy and a black child at school, the ones society deemed it safest to hate.

Maggie managed to find her way through a childhood filled with shame and anger into a relatively normal adulthood that was not without an undercurrent of fear.

Ken Mieske was not so lucky. Rejected by his family, he was living on the streets of Portland, Oregon, by the time he was fifteen. He bounced from bar to bar, from bedroom to bedroom, from street to prison, from one drug to another, trying to find some escape from pain and a place where he belonged.

Finally, Mieske found a group of black-booted, shaven-headed teenagers, a family of sorts. They had their own music, their own ideology, their own style. They had well-defined allegiances and clearly designated enemies. And they accepted him.

Among the Skinheads, Mieske found not only a place for himself but an outlet for all the frustration, fear, and anger of a lifetime spent as an outsider. His targets: the other outsiders—blacks, Jews, Asians, gays, and Latinos. If he was less than satisfied with his own life, he could at least feel superior to them. At last he had someone to blame. And he also had what in his culture had become an acceptable method of retaliation—brutal, random violence.

After Mieske broke his baseball bat on the skull of an Ethiopian man he had never seen before, killing him, the police asked him why. Why did he keep hitting the victim long after he was unable to fight back? Mieske answered, "I was mad."

And it was true. Mieske was filled with an anger that had no beginning and no end that he could imagine. Mieske was mad at life, and he chose to make others his victims. Perhaps he wasn't even aware of this.

Uncertain Ties

Social scientists have found that intolerant people come in all kinds: rich, poor, religious, nonreligious, educated, uneducated, male, female, Southern, Northern, American, European, children of bigots, and children of egalitarians. One study first conducted by Emory Bogardus and repeated over the years revealed, according to Thomas F. Pettigrew in *Prejudice,* "an amazingly consistent pattern of group prejudices . . . [that] varied little with the respondent's region, education, occupation, income, or even ethnicity."

The consistency of group prejudices points to the power of social stereotypes: those who are prejudiced are prejudiced in similar ways. What this study didn't measure, but other studies have tracked, is what differentiates those who are prejudiced from those who aren't.

In fact, only one difference between the tolerant and intolerant seems to have any significance, and that is the way they were treated as children in their families. The people who express the greatest intolerance had upbringings that robbed them of a safe and certain bond of love between themselves and their families.

The research on child development has been going on far longer than the research on prejudice, and it rarely produces a consensus on anything. But it has over the years resulted in nearly universal agreement on this: children need to know they are loved, no matter what. They need that knowledge immediately and they need it often. And if they don't get it, they are damaged.

Most works on child development emphasize this. One, Melvin Konner's *Childhood: A Multicultural View*, compares children of various societies and finds that the idea proposed by the psychoanalyst Erik Erikson in the early 1960s holds true for all people everywhere: "The main task of psychological development in the first two years of life is to form a trusting attitude toward the world and toward life itself. If you developed trust, you could rely on it for the rest of your life to help you pull through psychological challenges. If you didn't, you might be permanently plagued by insecurity, anxiety, and sadness."

Where does that trust come from? A host of studies with babies, toddlers, teenagers, and adults makes the answer clear: trust comes from Mom and Dad. John Bowlby summarized in *A Secure Base* the work of researchers Mary Ainsworth, Mary Main, and others whose observations and experiments have shown that babies whose signals (for feeding, changing, playing, comforting) are routinely noticed and responded to in the first six months of life become more attached to their parents. And children who are securely attached to their parents become more independent, more confident, and more caring adults.

The studies, Bowlby wrote, "leave no doubts . . . about what types of family experience influence development in one direction or another. Again and again we see details in the behavior of a toddler, or in what he says, that are plainly straight replicas of how that toddler has himself been treated. Indeed, the tendency to treat others in the same way that we ourselves have been treated is deep in human nature; and at no time is it more evident than in the earliest years."

The work of Gordon Allport confirms that prejudice develops when the needs for love, trust, and belonging are not met. He wrote: "Children brought up in a rejective home, exposed to ready-made prejudices, will scarcely be in a position to develop a trustful or affiliative outlook upon social relationships. Having received little affection, they are not in a position to give it."

Of course, the world is not made up of categories of people—the caring and indifferent, the loving and hateful, the tolerant and intolerant. All of us are each, more or less. Even prejudice cannot be stereotyped, because no single theory can encompass the complex, deeply interrelated, and often subtle influences that combine to make all human personalities. But we can learn something about how intolerance operates in our own lives by looking at these generalizations provided by the research:

Children who are loved and disciplined consistently, who feel free to express themselves and to try out new things, and children who see models of compassion around them are more likely to become independent, to make friends easily, to express compassion and empathy for strangers, and to feel comfortable in the world outside their families.

On the other hand, children raised by parents who are cold or erratic with their love, who are indifferent or abusive, who discipline harshly or inconsistently, are more likely to become insecure, distrustful, fearful, and lonely (and will in turn pass on similar problems to their children).

Not all of these children find expression for their insecurity in intolerance and hatred. For reasons we don't know, different people develop different ways of surviving lonely childhoods. Many take some other path of self-destruction, and the fortunate few are able to confront and transform their fears. But for people whose fears take hold in bigotry, prejudice becomes far more than a response to cultural norms or peer pressure. Rather, it is an intricate part of their personalities. They don't choose to be this way; they become this way because of how they've learned to survive in their families.

Studies of people with deeply held prejudices reveal certain common personality traits. Such people generally fear failure, are unable to cope with ambiguities, lack self-awareness, and have low self-esteem. They have little faith in themselves or in other people. Afraid and insecure, they construct a view of themselves and the world that most comfortably masks their feelings, disguises the ambiguities of the world, and gives them a false sense of belonging. Their entire personalities—their feelings, attitudes, and actions—are involved in a massive project of self-deception that distorts their view of the world and alienates them from other people and their own souls. Their lives become centered on the search for approval, the need for certainty, and the escape from self.

Behind the Hate

We are not all Ken Mieskes, but we have all experienced the feelings—insecurity, loneliness, fear, longing, frustration, and anger—that can lead to intolerance toward others. The feelings themselves are not wrong. They are universal. What matters is the influence we allow them to exert on our lives.

Those whose lives are marked by early and repeated rejection can become the unconscious captives of such emotions. Their bitterness, unacknowledged, destroys any chance for self-acceptance or for trusting relationships, and turns the world into a dangerous, threatening place that calls on all their defenses.

Among those defenses are the capacities for self-deception that can lead to prejudice and hatred—the tricks of categorization and generalization discussed in the last chapter. When we aim our hatred at a group of people we categorize as "the enemy," we view the members of that group not as human beings like us, but as part of a monstrous evil. Hatred becomes an obsession and provides us with a vision of the world that justifies our anger.

Some turn to hatred the way others turn to drugs to relieve their pain. "One can become addicted to hatred and therefore the target of hatred," wrote the sociologist Robert Jay Lifton. "One needs a target to go on hating and one needs hatred in order to feel alive."

Obsessive hatred usually finds its target in generalized groups of people rather than in specific individuals. We find it easier to reject people in large groups, clearly distinguishable from us by some obvious physical characteristic such as skin color, than we do to reject specific individuals who are, we must admit, more like us than not.

Mieske hated blacks. Senator McCarthy hated communists. Hitler hated Jews. Oswald hated capitalists. But first, they hated their own lives. They were the original victims of their own intolerance, but they didn't know it.

Hatred didn't heal them, of course. It never does. Hatred imprisons the one who hates. And while some of us, long ago labeled by social stereotypes, are more likely than others to be the victims of hatred, those who hate are likely to be any of us. Hatred is more discriminating in whom it targets than in whom it possesses. Given the right circumstances, we could all be Mieskes.

Toni Morrison's novel *The Bluest Eye* is peopled with characters who struggle against their own hate and the hatred of others. Cholly and Pauline and Pecola are sentenced by the color of their skin to live in a hateful world. Powerless to change their circumstances, they do not exit gracefully but struggle ferociously for some sense of worth. Cholly hides his humiliation in alcohol and anger and takes out his rage on women, especially the one closest to him, his wife. "She was one of the few things abhorrent to him that he could touch and therefore hurt," Morrison wrote. "He poured out on her the sum of all his inarticulate fury and aborted desires. Hating her, he could leave himself intact."

Mieske, too, found a sense of himself in hatred. It was the one emotion he could fully express, and by feeling it fully, he was momentarily made whole.

Broken Links

Hatred like Mieske's is just one form of intolerance. In fact, our everyday relations are more commonly handicapped not by hatred but by indifference. Often we simply don't notice the other person. We don't respond to her pain, we don't empathize with her needs, we don't concern ourselves with her problems, because we don't recognize ourselves in her. Somewhere along the way, we have lost the link that binds us to all people.

A blind boy rode my school bus throughout high school. Every day for three years he took his place on the seat behind the driver, and he always sat alone. He was bright, friendly. Everyone knew his name and lots of people said "hi," but no one was his friend. If we had given our indifference any thought, I suppose we might have reasoned that he was content to be alone. He smiled, he didn't demand attention, and he didn't sulk. He didn't see our rejection, we might have thought, so maybe he didn't feel it. But of course he did. He simply forgave us the blindness that was ours alone.

In the same way, many whites are indifferent to the perspectives of people of color. "Yes," they may say, "our ancestors were oppressive racists who victimized your ancestors. Yes, it's important to recognize the equal worth of all people. But we are not interested in actually listening to the anger you have, looking at the pain you've suffered, or participating in your struggles. We are sympathetic, of course. But we have lives of our own."

Many white people also continue to live with an assumption, mostly unrecognized, that their lives are not involved with the lives of minorities. Minorities, on the other hand, cannot help noticing hundreds of times a day how their lives are affected by white society. The indifference of white people is frustrating, but it's their unconsciousness of their own indifference that can be infuriating. Because they have not been forced to take seriously another perspective, regardless of how widespread that perspective is, they can effectively ignore it and feel no repercussions in their own lives.

And the indifference works both ways. Many minorities who have succeeded in spite of the obstacles are unwilling to take seriously the fears of a white blue-collar worker who believes he is a victim of an unfair system of preferences. It is easy to discount the pain of one who does not perceive your pain, and to justify indifference by the lines of politics and race that are firmly drawn between us.

Needing Approval

We are born with a desire for love, but we are not born loving ourselves. We have to learn how to do that if we are to become healthy, caring people. Having grown up without consistent care, interested attention, loving guidance, and regular affirmation, the habitually intolerant are forced to strive for some external affirmation of their worth to establish a secure place in the world. The greater their insecurity, the more urgent their need to prove themselves.

Paula was an attorney with a small firm in the Southern town where she was born and raised. She was active in her church and a member of the school board. She was considered a "liberal" by local standards, and she was proud of that. She had long ago rejected the racism of other Southern whites, including some members of her own family. She raised her two daughters to be tolerant. Then, one day, her oldest girl, a twenty-one-year-old college student who planned to go on to law school, introduced her to the African American man she was planning to marry.

Paula was shocked by her own reaction. As much as she wanted to be supportive, she was overcome with fear. At first she expressed her fears as concern for her child. How will she be treated? How will her children be treated? Her daughter did not share her concerns.

After many sleepless nights and tormented days, Paula decided to see a counselor. During the first session, as she was explaining her difficulty accepting the interracial marriage, she heard herself exclaim, "What will people think?" And she finally saw that the source of her fear was in herself, not in her daughter's decision. She was afraid that by welcoming a black son-in-law into the family, she would lose the approval of her church, her family, and her friends.

She began to see just how much she had relied on that approval to feel acceptable to herself. She had defined herself in terms of her social and economic success. Without her good job and her good standing in the community, she realized, she would be devastated. She saw that her insecurity had affected her judgments and decisions for a long time. And she recognized that the prejudice she was expressing against her daughter's marriage was rooted in her fears that she herself might not measure up to society's expectations. She decided to seek a solution to that fear, not by trying to change her daughter, but by changing herself.

We are all susceptible to feelings of superiority. According to Allport, for many people "the hunger for status is matched by a haunting fear that one's status may not be secure. The effort to maintain a precarious position can bring with it an almost reflex disparagement of others."

It is no secret who the "others" are: those who look different, live differently, or worship differently from the way we do. They may be *any* group of people we designate as not like "us." And we blame them for the inadequacies we feel in ourselves.

"Prejudiced people . . . practice self-hate unconsciously," wrote the psychologist B. K. Bryant. "Their failures and inadequacies become too great a burden for them to bear and, as a result, they turn their gaze outward to find an explanation. Thus, they target other people to serve as scapegoats. The degree of their self-hatred is likely reflected in the intensity of their hatred for the scapegoat group."

Our search for status takes many forms, but at its core is a desperate need to be recognized by others as a person of worth. Unable to find security within ourselves, we find it in the petty acts of aggression that somehow deceive us into feeling better. Because we cannot admit our own failures, we find others to blame them on. Because we feel inferior, we find others we can feel superior to. Because we are powerless over our insecurity, we attempt to control others. Because we are unable to laugh at ourselves, we laugh at others. Because we cannot allow weaknesses in ourselves, we cannot find help in others. Because we cannot accept ourselves as we are, we cannot accept others.

The extremely intolerant are skilled at condescension, distrust, blaming, and attention-getting. Defensiveness and arrogance are part of their personalities. They are strangers to the skills of forgiveness, compromise, trust, empathy, and open-mindedness. They are so obsessively focused on their own needs that they cannot give attention to the needs of others. They can't bear to think of themselves as wrong, weak, or inadequate. If they do not emerge victorious from every argument, if they cannot control other people, if they are cut from the team or bypassed for a job promotion, they are flooded with feelings of inadequacy, powerlessness, and even shame. For them to have any self-esteem at all, they must consider themselves stronger, smarter, and generally better than those around them.

In their desperation to establish themselves as people of value, they defeat their own purpose. They may rack up material rewards, even public praise, but true acceptance and belonging continue to elude them. The fact is, they have become unpleasant people to be around. People don't trust them and they are unable to trust other people. Their loneliness deepens, and the cycle of insecurity and animosity continues.

Seeking Certainty

Those who were raised without the assurance of love develop a suspicious outlook on the world and are compelled to try to control the events and circumstances of their lives. They cannot face the world as it is and people as they are, full of ambiguities. They cling to solid answers, clear-cut explanations, easy judgments, and quick decisions, no matter how mistaken they may be. While others may be able to brush off the normal confusions of life, they are terrified of them.

They are so uncomfortable with what they can't know that they construct a myth of certainty that defines the world in rigid measures of right and wrong, good and bad, success and failure. In search of mastery over their lives, they may turn to fundamentalist religions, the regimentation of a military life, or super-achieving careers. Unable to accept that people are complicated creatures who are sometimes good and sometimes bad, sometimes right and sometimes wrong, they quickly sort people into the "good" and "bad," "friend" and "enemy," and leave them there.

Very likely, this compulsion to categorize the world is part of the legacy of intolerance they received from parents who were themselves insecure and unable to show consistent love. And it is the same legacy they are likely to pass on to their children.

Many develop what psychologists call "authoritarian" personalities and a "threat orientation" toward life. Prejudiced people, studies have shown, tend to agree with statements like "The world is a hazardous place, where men are basically evil and dangerous." Deeply distrustful of their fellow humans, they try to impose order, if only in their minds, on the world around them.

The need for definiteness can be so strong that prejudiced people will go to great lengths to defend their misperceptions. In one experiment, two groups of people were asked to identify a very clear line drawing of a cat. "Cat," people in both groups answered correctly. Then they were asked to identify a series of further drawings by which the cat was slowly transformed into a dog. Tolerant people answered "I don't know" when the drawings began to change. But prejudiced people insisted that what they were seeing was a cat, even when it was indecipherable.

The need for certainty is at the root of another common characteristic of prejudiced personalities: the inability to handle frustration. Numerous experimental studies show that prejudiced people are much more likely to become frustrated, resentful, and angry when confronted with a problem. In one study cited by Thomas Pettigrew, "highly anti-Semitic college women increased their hostility toward an innocent peer when annoyed by an experimenter, while more tolerant women actually became friendlier."

The social scientists based their findings on studies of people who expressed strong and consistent prejudices (even though they were often not aware that they were doing so). Those of us whose prejudice is less life-consuming may not rely on our emotional defenses to the extremes described above, but we do find comfort in them from time to time.

We are saved from self-destruction if we recognize these misguided attempts to find security.

The Loss of Self

The habits of intolerance, when they become part of our personality, don't exist in isolation from other traits. They are embedded in an entire personality structure that we may develop to protect our fragile image of ourselves. It's an inadequate, unhealthy structure, and it survives only so long as we don't look at it. Ultimately, a life of prejudice, fear, and insecurity can hold together only by being faithfully ignored. It is a lonely, painful, self-destructive existence no one would envy.

Prejudice is usually a hidden affliction; those who suffer from it generally don't know why they hurt or how they hurt others. "To admit prejudice is to accuse oneself of being both irrational and unethical. No one wants to be at odds with his own conscience. Man has to live with himself," Allport wrote. "The sufferer is not aware of the psychological function that prejudice serves in his life."

To hide from our own prejudices, we must deny part of ourselves. It is no wonder, then, that intolerant people have great difficulty seeing themselves as they are. Intensive studies of anti-Semites during the 1940s, according to Pettigrew, found that "central to the syndrome is anti-intraception, the refusal to look inside oneself and the lack of insight into one's own behavior and feelings."

Afraid of what they might find, the intolerant shut their eyes to their own souls and live as outsiders to themselves. They have a firm and inflexible idea of who they must be in order to be accepted, and they have learned early on to ignore, deny, or project onto others every facet of their being that displeases them. People who hate themselves, said the psychologist Thomas J. Cottle, "don't go looking for themselves."

This lack of self-perception is an indispensable trick of extreme bigotry. If they knew why they targeted certain groups for hatred, the haters would no longer be able to hate successfully. So they blind themselves to the ways their attitudes and behavior affect other lives. They don't see the true source of their frustrations and fears. Their fragile self-images won't abide examination. For everything they feel is wrong with their lives—and there is much to despair over—they must find others to blame. The easiest scapegoats are the faceless, nameless crowds of people that society has tagged the "outsiders."

Self-reflection

There is an escape from the prison of fear and prejudice. It begins very simply with an honest look in the mirror. Once we see ourselves as we are, the reality appears in sharp contrast to the values we hold. Though we may believe prejudice to be wrong, we are nevertheless sometimes unfair in our judgments of others. While we want to be generous in our relationships, we discover that we are frequently quite selfish.

Acknowledging the conflict between our values and our actions is extremely uncomfortable and is likely to be followed by a desire for change. The anthropologist Mary Catherine Bateson has likened this self-discovery to culture shock—the discombobulation we feel when confronted with unfamiliar ways. "Losing the certainty of a particular worldview [or self-image] can make you feel sick, bewildered, dizzy," she wrote. "In severe culture shock, one may feel that one is going insane."

Dealing with the shock of self-discovery requires a willingness to learn new ways of thinking and being. When self-discovery reveals a habitual intolerance, the motivation to change is enhanced by guilt and confusion. Our rationalizations and generalizations of intolerance no longer work, because we can see through them. We strive to reconcile our attitudes and behavior with our values because we cannot be at peace with ourselves otherwise. Only when we can examine ourselves honestly, and find some satisfaction in who we are, can we finally look at the people around us with a more generous heart.

This is where the journey from intolerance to tolerance begins: with a good hard look in the mirror. This is not an easy process and it cannot be accomplished overnight. It requires a vigilant and fearless honesty, a willingness to endure the pain that self-awareness brings, and a faith that change is possible.

∽

JOURNAL NOTES
CHAPTER 3

1. Myself, the outsider. We have all been outsiders at one time or another. Recall a time you felt apart from the group. Describe yourself from a third-person perspective, as if you were looking at the scene from a distance. What did you look like? How did you move, talk, and act? What did you seem to feel? How were others treating you? If you could change the picture you see, what would it look like?

What are some of the stereotypes that you think people sometimes apply to you? How do you react to those stereotypes?

2. Indifference. You walked by a homeless person on the street. Where did you focus your eyes? What did you notice about that person? What did you think of him? How did you feel as you walked by?

3. Insecurity. Under what circumstances do you feel self-conscious? What is it about yourself that makes you insecure?

4. Proving myself. List some of the ways you have recently sought approval from others.

5. Hatred. Describe someone you've hated: her personality, behavior, and looks. What do you hate most about that person? Now, describe yourself as a person who hates. What do you look like? How do you talk? How do you feel?

Changes

Each separate being in the universe
returns to the common source.
Returning to the source is serenity.
If you don't realize the source,
you stumble in confusion and sorrow.
When you realize where you come from,
you naturally become tolerant . . .
LAO-TZU

In the beginning of our children's lives, we are the world. If we are angry, their world is a fearful, threatening place. If we are sullen and distracted, their world is lonely. If we are erratic in our attentions, loving and unreachable by turns, the world is terrifyingly unpredictable.

How can we offer a child security if we are insecure?

How can we offer them love if we feel unloved? Can we laugh and play with them if we are un' ppy? Where do we find patience with them in the m' . of our anger? How do we listen to them when we preoccupied with our own worries?

If children wer ss perceptive creatures, we might try pretense. But th see beyond our superficial words and gestures. Ulti ely, whether we know it or not, we give our childre whatever is deepest in our characters. And this is wha they take to heart.

When we have the courage to face ourselves in any circumstance, when we can feel comfortable with ourselves despite our shortcomings, when we can enjoy our lives, then we become parents capable of a love that's certain. We can offer our children the sense of security they need to become caring and involved in the world around them.

Part of parenting is being prepared for growth and change—our own as well as our children's. When we receive our children into the world, we are given an opportunity for personal exploration that can guide us toward a greater acceptance of ourselves and others. Certainly, if we wish to prepare our children for lives of happiness and tolerance, we cannot avoid this exploration. Our relationship with our children can be the model for tolerance in our lives.

The very idea of change is daunting. Our thoughts, feelings, and actions are old habits, and we don't alter them easily. But what's most difficult about change is not the change itself. What's difficult is being honest about who we are to begin with. Once we can face ourselves as we are, letting go of resentments about our past and fears for our future, once we can take responsibility for our own lives, then change happens.

Seeing Ourselves

An Iroquois named Man Who Eats Humans was sitting at home over his steaming supper kettle one day when he saw the reflection of a face in the simmering water. He recognized it, but he didn't recognize it. The features seemed to be his own, but there was something distinctively wise and noble about the appearance. "I didn't know I was like that," he said to himself. From that moment on, he quit eating people for supper and instead became a messenger of peace to the warring Iroquois nations. His new name was Hiawatha.

It is perhaps the hardest thing we have to do—seeing ourselves clearly, as we are. Self-awareness, in fact, begins with discomfort. Researchers have found that babies, when they first begin to recognize the image in the mirror as themselves, react with confusion and consternation. Even as adults, we are startled when we see our faces on a department store's video screen, or when we hear our voices played on tape. Is that the way I look? Is that the way I sound?

In his last book of essays, the novelist Walker Percy reflected on the inability of humans to sustain an accurate image of themselves. "A person who looks at a group picture looks for himself first: everyone else in the picture looks more or less as he knew they would—they are what they are;

but he does not know what he is, and so he looks to see; and when he finds himself, he always experiences a slight pang: so that is who I am! But this formulation is ephemeral, and he will do the same thing with the next group picture."

It requires great courage to stare into the stew of our mistakes, to see all our pain and rage and fear come boiling to the surface. But if we look long enough, unblinkingly, we are able, like Hiawatha, to discern a deeper reflection of a good person. And we become capable of change.

When we can acknowledge the good in ourselves, along with the deep contradictions in our characters, we take the first step toward tolerance. As it turns out, we are not unlike those we envy; we are not unlike those we despise. We are simply good people who sometimes act horribly. Our eyes open to our own humanity; we see more clearly the humanity in others. We begin to perceive the deep connections we have to all others and to feel responsible for those connections. In the simple act of recognizing ourselves, we find that we do indeed belong.

There is no telling how many pots of misery Man Who Eats Humans watched boil before he was granted an image of kindness. For most of us, such a transformation comes slowly. Sometimes, it is only after many painful encounters with our own contradictions ("when the dissatisfaction is great enough," as Allport wrote), that we see ourselves and then see ourselves in others.

Requirements of Change

Jake G. is a white, middle-aged tattooed biker who spent a good part of his life hating blacks, Jews, and gays, and demonstrating his hate through violence. He found countless excuses to attack those he didn't like. He even killed a man in a blind rage. His family life fell apart, and finally he wound up in prison. There, he joined the Aryan Brotherhood, a white supremacist prison gang, and encountered more fights, more hatred, and more trouble. It was not until he joined Narcotics Anonymous that he was able to take an honest look at himself. What he discovered, he says, was that his hatred and anger were hurting him.

Jake's recovery group was made up of diverse people—including whites, Latinos, blacks, Jews, and gays—who all happened to be searching for a life free from drugs and alcohol. As a member of that group, Jake discovered that his deepest feelings, hopes, and dreams were shared by the very people he used to hate. He describes the journey toward tolerance as a process of learning first about himself and discovering, to his great surprise, that he was, in the most important ways, just like everyone else. He puts it bluntly: "It took me a long time to figure out that the skin you come wrapped in don't mean shit."

What Jake required, what most of us require, to change our ways of thinking about and dealing with other people, is a way of seeing ourselves clearly. It so happened that because of his drug addiction Jake was led into one of the most effective and practical methods of personal change available: a twelve-step recovery program.

M. Scott Peck, in his book *Further Along the Road Less Traveled*, has called the founding of Alcoholics Anonymous, the basis of all twelve-step programs, "the greatest positive event of the twentieth century . . . It was not only the beginning of the self-help movement and the beginning of the integration of science and spirituality at a grass-roots level, but also the beginning of the community movement."

Today, through various "Anonymous" programs, millions of people have been able to overcome what seemed to them insurmountable crises, and they have made changes they never thought possible. What most program participants have found is that their personal freedom depends, in part, on their ability to deal with life as it is, and to accept themselves and others as they are.

Tolerance, they have learned, comes only when they are able to apply the principles of honesty, open-mindedness, and willingness in their lives. By being fearlessly honest about ourselves, we realize that we have faults, that we make mistakes, that we hurt others, and that there is much we don't know. Once we have that realization, we cannot help recognizing that we are much like the people we don't like— and in just the ways we don't like about them. With that recognition comes humility. We have to accept in ourselves the things we have found it so hard to accept in others, and we forgive others for their failures, knowing that we, too, are capable of the same mistakes.

Open-mindedness comes more easily after we have honestly admitted our faults. We know now that we don't have all the answers, that our way of life is not by any means perfect, and we become open to other ideas, other ways of living. We are able to listen to others, honoring the differences between us and empathizing with the feelings that are also ours.

Neither honesty nor open-mindedness can last for long, though, unless we are willing to take the steps necessary for change. This means practicing tolerance even when we don't think or feel tolerant, with the faith that our actions will help reform our hearts and minds. The writer Wendell Berry, in *The Hidden Wound,* examined the racist roots of his own prejudices and concluded that for individuals to learn tolerance, "to know and come to care for one another," they must bring themselves "face to face, arduously, and by the willing loss of comfort."

The Loss of Comfort

Studs Terkel's oral history *Race* contains the story of one man's uncomfortable journey toward tolerance.

C. P. Ellis was a gun-toting, robe-wearing officer in the local chapter of the Ku Klux Klan when the civil rights movement came to Durham, North Carolina. He refused to shake the hand of a black person and wouldn't think of sitting down at the same table with one. He once held a young black man at gunpoint and threatened to kill him.

Ann Atwater, an African American woman, was at the forefront of civil rights demonstrations in Durham. She led a series of successful black boycotts against downtown businesses that discriminated against blacks. She didn't like white people. She didn't trust them, and she didn't talk to them.

When a communitywide meeting was called to study racial problems in the Durham schools, C. P. Ellis and Ann Atwater were both there. C.P. told the crowd, "If we didn't have niggers in the schools, we wouldn't have the problems we have today." During the next meeting, a human relations committee was named to help ease racial tensions. It would be chaired by C. P. Ellis and Ann Atwater. After the initial horror passed, they both agreed.

What resulted was, for Ellis in particular, a personal transformation from hate to acceptance and even love.

Ellis had grown up poor, the son of a man who worked hard, drank heavily, and died young. Ellis went through school ashamed of his poverty, humiliated by the constant teasing he took about his raggedy clothes. He left school in the eighth grade, when his father died, so that he could support the family.

It wasn't long before he found himself repeating his father's life. "I worked my butt off and never seemed to break even . . . I began to say there's somethin' wrong with this country. I really began to get bitter . . . I had to hate somebody . . . The natural person for me to hate would be black people, because my father before me was a member of the Klan."

In a room full of white-robed, like-minded men, C.P.

found his place. "I can understand why people join extreme right-wing or left-wing groups," he said. "They're in the same boat I was in. Shut out. Deep down inside, we want to be part of this great society."

With his gun, his robe, and a target for his hatred, C.P. began to feel he had a goal in life beyond making ends meet. Still, "I'd go home at night and wrestle with myself. I'd look at a black person walkin' down the street and the guy'd have ragged shoes or his clothes would be worn. That began to do somethin' to me inside."

When he was named to the human relations committee, C.P. felt a new sense of belonging, a chance to be somebody. But his old friends told him he was selling out the white race. "This began to make me have guilty feelin's."

The beginning of self-awareness is always scary, because the old tricks of denial and projection begin to fail. Once embarked on the journey of self-discovery, we find that we learn things whether we want to or not. Something new began happening in C.P.'s life. "All of a sudden [I'm] tryin' to deal with my feelin's, my heart. My mind was beginnin' to open up. I was beginnin' to see what was right and what was wrong."

C.P. and Ann Atwater met regularly, struggling uncomfortably to find solutions to the community's racial tensions. Then one day Ann told C.P. that her daughter had come home from school crying because the teacher made fun of her. Ann was worried and hurt, and C.P. understood her pain. A white teacher had made fun of his own son because C.P. was a Klansman. In that moment, C.P. and Ann both cried, and "I begin to see, here we are, two people from the far ends of the fence, havin' identical problems, except her bein' black and me bein' white. From that moment on, I tell ya, that gal and I worked together good. I begin to love the girl."

Ellis began his journey with the willingness to work with someone he didn't feel like working with, the courage to confront himself, and the open-mindedness to recognize his own pain in the pain of someone he thought he hated.

The poet Maya Angelou also came to tolerance through pain. She had learned well, early on, whom to look down upon, whom to fear, and whom to hate. Her hatred of white people, born as it was from repeated mistreatment by them, was not surprising. But she reached a point when she knew she could not continue to hate and survive. As a temporarily homeless teenager, she spent a month living in a junk yard in the company of other homeless youths—black, Mexican, and white. She learned dance steps from a Mexican boy and sold empty bottles with a white girl, and she came to understand that her own survival depended on group cooperation.

"After a month," she wrote in *I Know Why the Caged Bird Sings*, "my thinking processes had so changed that I was hardly recognizable to myself. The unquestioning acceptance by my peers had dislodged the familiar insecurity. Odd that the homeless children . . . could initiate me into the brotherhood of man . . . I was never again to sense myself so solidly outside the pale of our human race."

People of Value

All who change—including Angelou and Ellis, Hiawatha and Jake G.—must find inside themselves hope and self-confidence, the feeling that though they have made mistakes and carried grave misconceptions, they are still valuable, and still capable of change. The journeys just described would have ended in misery and isolation if the travelers had not walked through the pain of self-reflection toward self-acceptance.

In Cormac McCarthy's novel *All the Pretty Horses,* a girl with a deformed hand resists the friendship of a boy with a glass eye, out of embarrassment and insecurity, until one night when he talks to her about "how he had lost his eye and of the cruelty of the children at his school . . . He said that those who have endured some misfortune will always be set apart but that it is just that misfortune which is their gift and which is their strength and that they must make their way back into the common enterprise of man for without they do so it cannot go forward and they themselves will wither in bitterness . . . I wanted very much to be a person of value and I had to ask myself how this could be possible if there were not something like a soul or like a spirit that is in the life of a person and which could endure any misfortune or disfigurement and yet be not less for it. If one were to be a person of value that value could not be a condition subject to the hazards of fortune. It had to be a quality that could not change. No matter what."

That "something like a soul or like a spirit" does not need to be defined. But it must be found if we are to have faith enough to believe that change is possible. Each of the "Anonymous" recovery programs relies on the same twelve steps for growth, all of which lead to self-discovery through reliance on a power greater than ourselves. That power may be called "spirit," "love," "God," or any other name. Those who have found it know that language can't contain or describe it. "It" is whatever gives us hope, strength, and security through the hard times, whatever allows us to reach inside to our deepest selves and reach out toward others in honesty and love. For some, the power greater than ourselves may lie in humanity's ancient ideals of human relationships—fairness, compassion, respect—principles that everyone shares but that no one can perfectly embody.

Becoming tolerant is all about healing relationships— our relationship to ourselves included. This healing doesn't come overnight, and it doesn't come without pain. But it is possible. The most difficult thing is not working toward change, but acknowledging that change is needed in the first place. We must face the fact of our intolerance and have faith in our own ability to change. It's no coincidence that in the first two steps of all twelve-step programs people are asked to deal with their denial and disbelief.

There is no organization of "intolerants anonymous." Most people enter these programs only when facing an uncontrollable, life-threatening crisis, when they have "hit bottom." They find themselves trapped in situations where denial is no longer possible. They cannot but realize that they have a problem. Regardless of the specific problem, however, most recovering people discover that intolerance in some form is another problem in their lives—one that, unchecked, can lead to disastrous places. The very goal they're striving for in recovery, to become content with themselves and others, requires them to learn tolerance.

We don't have to hit the "bottom" of despair and confusion to benefit from the tools for tolerance that such programs teach. Of those tools, the most well-known is the Serenity Prayer. All over the world, twelve-step meetings begin with a group recitation of Reinhold Niebuhr's prayer, which is itself a plea for tolerance: *Grant me the serenity to accept what I cannot change, the courage to change the things I can, and the wisdom to know the difference.*

The other tools are a series of simple, practical suggestions for personal change that have given millions of people a new way to live.

Looking in the Mirror

Self-awareness, the beginning of all change, is at the heart of the twelve-step programs. Taking a personal inventory requires more than thinking about ourselves; it requires writing about ourselves and talking about ourselves with others who care. The inventory is the first step toward tolerance.

If we're honest, we don't have to look far to recognize the intolerance in our lives. We fail to accept people as they are whenever we try manipulating someone to think what we want him to think, act the way we want him to act, or feel what we want him to feel. We consider ourselves superior whenever we criticize someone's character. We stereotype people whenever we put someone into a category or type based on appearance. We are prejudiced whenever we make judgments about someone without knowing her personally. We are unforgiving whenever we hold anger and resentment against someone. Whenever we do these things, and whenever we hate or ignore other people, we are being intolerant.

We must admit to ourselves that our intolerance has hurt us as well as others. It may take a little effort to realize this, because we often believe that our intolerant reactions are reasonable, appropriate to the circumstances, and even unavoidable.

To understand how our intolerance harms us, we recall several recent occasions when we were intolerant in some way and we put them down in writing. We list the specific types of intolerance we expressed: "I was (condescending, judgmental, disrespectful, mean, insensitive, hateful, cold, prejudiced)." Then we describe our actions: "When I (told X they were x, or when I said x about X)." We identify our feelings before, during, and after the incident, simply by listing them, without trying to explain them. Then we describe how we were harmed by our behavior. How did we feel about ourselves? How did we feel toward others? How did it change our relationships with others?

By separating our actions from our feelings, we discover that the harm we have done is most often rooted in our own insecurities and fears. The more we learn to recognize the feelings in ourselves, the less compelled we are to act on them.

But recognizing that intolerance is a part of us does not rid us of it. We can't change ourselves by ourselves. Our habits of thinking, our emotional reactions, and our feelings about ourselves have been an integral part of our personalities for many years. Regardless of how hard we try to act, think, and feel differently in any given situation, we find the old patterns reasserting themselves. If we truly desire change, we must find help.

The help we seek can be found in the enduring power of humane ideals. The principles of tolerance have been revered by humanity through many generations, and their evidence is all around us. We can find them in the poetry, fiction, history, scripture, and dance of many cultures and many eras. We can hear them in popular songs and everyday conversation. We can see them being acted on in our own communities. Of course, we also see plenty of evidence of intolerance. What's important is that, collectively, we know there is a better way to live together. Whatever we believe about the source of humane ideals, they have been proven to have power and endurance beyond all human attempts to destroy them. Despite how we act toward one another, we all know, and have forever known, how we would *like* to act. That in itself is something miraculous.

With the faith that change is possible, we continue to take inventory. Building on the first few incidents we mentioned earlier, we set about describing every act of intolerance that we can remember committing. We leave the other person's actions out of it. We don't offer justifications for our behavior. Then we list the feelings we imagine the other person had as a result of our behavior. If we don't know, we describe how we would feel had we been in her place. And we list the feelings we had that were related to our behavior. This step is tedious and sometimes painful, but patience and pain are prerequisites for personal growth. The benefits we gain from self-discovery are well worth the discomfort.

We have named our acts of intolerance; now we need to claim them. We need to tell one other person what we have discovered about ourselves. By fully admitting our failures, we learn humility, self-acceptance, and we begin to forgive ourselves. When we admit who we are, we are bound to feel some disappointment and regret, but when we confess it to another human being, that disappointment is relieved. Speaking out loud to someone we trust is discovering that we are not horrendous; we're just not perfect. We're human. In fact, we have a great deal more in common with other people than we imagined. It's important that we take this step with someone who will be nonjudgmental, who will fully honor our confidentiality, and who understands clearly our reasons for doing this.

To accept ourselves, we must let go of our past and forgive ourselves the wrongs we've done. If we are honest in the examination of our lives, we find that we sometimes violated our own most basic values in our attempts to get what we wanted. We feel guilty, which is quite reasonable. But we know that our ultimate goal is to like ourselves, shortcomings and all, and we cannot accomplish that as long as we hang on to our guilt and regrets. The forgiveness of other people is not enough. We have to forgive ourselves.

The best way to earn our own forgiveness is to make amends to people we have harmed. We list those people and we offer apologies and restitution where possible, but we refrain from reopening old wounds and exposing ourselves to danger. We don't expect anything in return. These people may or may not forgive us; they may suspect our motives or simply be baffled by our amends. That does not matter. We make amends for ourselves, to clear out the damage of our past so that we can move on to a new future.

Doing the Footwork

To continue the process of self-acceptance and tolerance, we make a habit of looking honestly at our daily lives and admitting when we are intolerant toward others in thought or deed. And we begin trying to do things differently. Generally, this means vigilantly exercising a self-discipline far stricter than we had bargained for. It means engaging in the tedious process of reminding ourselves to refrain from old behaviors and to practice new ones.

We cannot become tolerant in isolation. If we are serious about overcoming our intolerant habits, we must actively reach out to others whom we would normally avoid. We must intentionally cross racial, religious, and economic bounds, and take the risk of entering each other's lives for the purpose of discovering some connection between us. Ultimately, the solution to intolerance can be found only in the context of our relationships. We need others, we need family, friends, and those we had deemed strangers, to mirror us to ourselves, to help us practice change.

In time, with practice, we begin to experience comfort and security with ourselves and satisfaction with those around us. We become able to take responsibility for all our actions and to forgive ourselves. We become less dependent on the approval of others to guide our lives. We realize that we can choose how to live our lives. And we become comfortable in the habit of examining ourselves, allowing new discoveries to lead toward further change.

When tolerance comes naturally, we aren't compelled to criticize those we disagree with or to gossip about the way others choose to live. When problems occur, we can look first to ourselves and ask what part we are playing. We can distinguish between what is our responsibility and what is not. We can see where our own lives end and where the other, separate, lives around us begin.

For parents, this last lesson is particularly important. Becoming tolerant, we can accept the limitations of our influence on our children and understand how best to guide them. We learn, in the process of getting to know ourselves, that we can never perfectly model the values we want our children to practice.

Fortunately, guiding our children toward tolerance does not require that we always be tolerant. It does necessitate that we remain firmly convinced of the value of tolerance, articulate that value with sensitivity and sincerity, be aware when we violate that value, and share with our children our efforts, past and present, to incorporate tolerance into our own lives.

Certainly we can demonstrate to our children the superficial expressions of civility, politeness, and diplomacy, but unless we guide them through the real moral struggles of our lives and theirs, we are not giving them the stronger, essential tools of community. When we allow them to experience and witness in us the difficult paths toward clarity, compromise, and forgiveness, with all the pain and confusion that are involved, we show them the way toward tolerance. This requires a willingness to see ourselves as we are and to envision the people that we might become.

Ultimately, we cannot predict how our children will feel about themselves, how they will view the world, or how they will relate to others. But we do know, from our own experience and a vast amount of research, that the answers to these questions lie in the relationships we build between ourselves and our children. Once we have grown comfortable with seeing ourselves for who we are, we can offer our children the gifts they need to be comfortable with themselves and with all kinds of others. Considering what we know about our own human nature, it is no surprise that what our children need most from us are secure bonds of love, consistent compassionate guidance, and models of moral behavior. With these gifts—love, guidance, example—we lead them toward tolerance. And the greatest gift is love.

⤳

JOURNAL NOTES
CHAPTER 4

1. **Review your journal notes and begin your inventory of intolerance.** Follow the guidelines described in "Looking in the Mirror" (page 72). Pay special attention to the times you felt guilty, inadequate, lonely, fearful, insecure, angry, or ashamed in relation to others.

2. **Describe yourself.** List the intolerant traits you have, using Chapters 2 and 3 and your journal notes as references. List your tolerant traits.

3. **Share yourself.** Talk about the intolerance in your life with a trusted friend, a member of the clergy, or a support group.

4. **Forgive yourself.** Write a "Dear Me" letter, offering empathy, understanding, and forgiveness for the wrongs you've done.

5. **Imagine change.** Write a description of your best self.

6. **Make a commitment.** Write a specific plan of action for situations that are likely to trigger intolerant feelings in

you. Describe the situation, what your typical response would be, and what your new response will be. Follow that plan to the best of your ability.

7. **Practice change.** Monitor your interactions with others. Take notice of when you are controlling, judgmental, condescending, defensive, cold, and hateful. List the behaviors you most want to change, and practice recognizing them. Then, as you begin to recognize your urge to act intolerantly, practice refraining from the behaviors. As your ability to refrain grows, so will your degree of self-acceptance.

Bonds
of Belonging

*We are born helpless. As soon as we are
fully conscious we discover loneliness. We
need others physically, emotionally,
intellectually; we need them if we are to
know anything, even ourselves.*
C. S. Lewis

Leah Hager Cohen grew up at the school for the deaf where
her mother and father worked, and for a long time she considered it a great misfortune that she could hear. She put
pebbles in her ears to mimic the hearing aids some children
wore. She pretended not to hear when people talked aloud.
When she talked to herself, she used sign language, forming
the words quickly and secretively in her lap. And when the
deaf children in her class listened to a story through ampli-

fied headphones, Leah sat alone, without headphones or hearing aid, listening to her teacher read the story. "I never felt so apart," she wrote in *Train Go Sorry*. "The privilege of being able to hear paled in comparison to the privilege of being close, of sharing that common experience with the other children."

What Leah felt as a hearing child in a deaf community was the inevitable struggle of one who is different, trying to be the same, trying to belong. So much of what we do and how we think is guided by our need to find a comfortable place for ourselves in the world. Whether or not we find that security has a great impact on how well we are able to accept other people. Indeed, Gordon Allport has suggested that "the development of mature and democratic personalities is largely a matter of building inner security."

And that inner security is born at home. The love of family first tells us that we are not alone, that we belong. The stronger the bond of love at home, the safer and more inviting the rest of the world seems. And differences, when they are encountered, become more interesting than threatening.

The relationship of family bonds to attitudes of tolerance has been well established by studies of tolerant and intolerant personalities. Those people most likely to be open-minded and empathic toward others share the experience of having been raised in homes where bonds of love were strong and lasting.

One study cited by Allport compared fourth-, fifth-, and sixth-graders who expressed prejudiced attitudes with those who didn't, and asked their mothers to respond to detailed questionnaires. The study found that parent-child relationships based on power rather than on unconditional love were more likely to lead children toward intolerance.

A study of German men who had resisted Nazism found, according to Allport, that "their mothers were more than usually demonstrative in their affection," and that there was a "sense of early and basic security" in their family relationships. A similar study of non-Jews who helped Jews escape the Nazis found that, compared with those who remained bystanders, the rescuers had close relationships with both parents and, according to James Q. Wilson in *The Moral Sense,* had extended their "warm familial feelings" to others; they "saw people as basically good and had many close friends."

These findings are consistent with similar observations throughout psychology. Dr. M. Scott Peck observed, for instance, that children who are reared in warm and loving homes are able to leave those homes more easily than those reared in cold and hostile homes. "Logically," he wrote, "the opposite should have held true . . . But gradually it dawned on me that the experience of their home life tends to shape children's visions of the world." Children from loving homes feel the world to be a friendly place and are eager to see more of it. Children from hostile environments are terrified of what the world may be and seek to avoid it.

The interesting thing about this discovery is that it doesn't much matter what the specific forms of our child-rearing practices look like. What matters is that we respond in some way to our children's universal need to be loved and cared for. A Navajo baby is swaddled tightly and strapped to a cradle board. A !Kung baby is held constantly, nursed frequently, and sleeps by her mother's side. A child of middle-class Americans is talked to all the time but may cry herself to sleep in a crib. Babies born on an Israeli kibbutz are handed over to a communal caretaker for most of the day. Yet in all of these cultures, babies learn to smile at about the same time; they begin to cry at their mothers' absence at about the same age; they communicate with sounds and words at about the same time.

"On the whole it is amazing that quite normal adults can arise from very different childhoods," observed Melvin Konner, in *Childhood: A Multicultural View*. The routines of a baby's life in one country may bear little resemblance to a baby's life on the other side of the planet, but it can be a happy, secure life as long as he knows there are people he can depend on.

Despite the vast differences in parenting practices, the research tells us that if our children are to become confident, caring people, all of them need certain things from the start. They need our presence: we must be with them. They need our attention: we must be aware of their feelings and concerns. And they need our care: we must respond reliably to their needs. These are the most basic requirements for building a secure bond with our children, and they are the essential duties of all parents everywhere.

Penelope Leach, the British pediatrician, wrote, "Every time a baby's very existence is celebrated in another spontaneous hug; every time her sounds, expressions, and body language are noticed and answered, a tiny piece is added to the foundations of that baby's future self-image, self-confidence, and social competence."

For parents who particularly want to give their children the tools for tolerance in a world of diversity, it is vitally important that the bonds they form be characterized by just those skills the children are to learn: empathy, respect, acceptance, forgiveness, and involvement. By practicing these skills, we not only strengthen the family bonds our children need; we offer them the models of tolerance they need to develop these skills themselves.

Empathy

He prayed—it wasn't my religion.
He ate—it wasn't what I ate.
He spoke—it wasn't my language.
He dressed—it wasn't what I wore.
He took my hand—it wasn't the color of mine.
But when he laughed—it was
how I laughed, and when he cried—
it was how I cried.

In her poem, sixteen-year-old Amy Maddox of Bargers-ville, Indiana, expressed the deepest connections possible between two human beings. To know that another feels what I feel is to know that I am not alone in the world, that I can find something of myself in others, even those who appear to be very different from me.

Empathy is what allows us to make those connections. All that's required is that we accurately perceive another's feelings and imagine feeling the same way ourselves. It's possible for us to empathize with people we've never met, with people we don't necessarily like, with other species of animals, even with characters in a movie.

We are born with the capacity for empathy. Newborns cry at the sound of another child's cry more frequently than they cry at a recording of their own cry or a computer-simulated cry, the studies of the social psychologist Martin L. Hoffman show. Hoffman, quoted in Morton Hunt's *The Compassionate Beast*, reported that such crying may be "empathic arousal," the "innate response out of which empathy is later developed." Another series of experiments, by Carolyn Zahn-Waxler at the National Institute of Mental Health, showed that one-year-olds are capable of offering comfort to adults who display hurt.

We grow more or less empathic very quickly. By the age of two, some children are compelled to comfort others in distress, and others aren't. We don't fully know why some people are more responsive to the feelings of another, but research has provided some clues about human empathy. People who are secure and self-confident are more likely to reach out to others. They trust their own assessment of the other's predicament and they are not afraid of the other's reaction. And because they are not preoccupied with their own fears, they can see clearly the feelings and needs of another. Also, people who have experienced empathy in their close relationships are more able to react with empathy toward others.

Like tolerance, empathy requires us to perceive others fearlessly, as they are, to recognize the heart of another as akin to ours. Empathy requires an understanding that all people share the same emotions—that whatever you are feeling, I am capable of feeling also. And empathy comes more easily when we accept that those emotions are manifested differently in different people at different times, when we recognize their feelings as real even though we would not react the same way in those circumstances.

This is easier, of course, when we've actually experienced such feelings. That's where adults have a distinct advantage over children. Everything our children feel, we have felt before, yet we often react as though we don't understand their feelings. A toy gets broken, a doll is lost, a friend refuses to share, a request for candy is denied, and our child wails at top volume. For us, the explosion of feeling seems wildly disproportionate to the circumstances. We would like the child to feel different, to be quiet, to accept the loss with grace and good cheer. We become impatient, angry, even disgusted at the "childish" response, and our hostility heightens the child's pain.

Though a child may respond quite differently from an adult to a given situation, the feelings he expresses are real. His sadness is no different from our sadness; his anger is just like ours. We may not be able to change his feelings, but we are obligated to accept them and try to understand them.

Building trust and inviting communication with a child means putting ourselves in the child's place. This we can't do unless we have a fairly good idea about who we are. The retired kindergarten teacher Vivian Paley for many years thought and wrote about how adults can come to know and accept children as they are. "We are not connected to one another by accumulations of skills and facts," she writes, "but, rather, by inner fears and fantasies, impulsive urges and pleasures. That which every child feels we all feel; that which every child fears we all fear. The challenge is to uncover what *we* feel and fear and fantasize and desire, so we may proceed toward the understanding of another person."

To build connections with children, Paley continues, "we must first pin ourselves down to certain memories and make conscious certain kinds of behaviors. It will be necessary to recall how we felt as children . . . What is it that makes us or has made us feel most frighteningly alone? How do we feel when we do not know or have forgotten that which we are supposed to know, when people seem to ignore or dislike us, when we are caught doing something that is *not nice?* How do we behave when we are angry?"

When we can recognize in the child's behavior how we once reacted, our response is likely to be generous, understanding, and instructive. Once empathy arrives, words of comfort and acts of caring quickly follow.

For us to empathize with our children, we must be able to do certain things:

1. Pay attention. Listen to what children are saying. Watch their body movements and facial expressions.
2. Identify the feelings at work in their words and actions.
3. Remember a time when we felt the same way.
4. Let our children know that what they are feeling, we have also felt. Share our own experiences and offer hope.

When someone lets us know he understands, we feel free to express our own feelings. In the same way, by letting a child know we understand his feelings because we've felt them ourselves, we invite openness and honesty. We offer a valuable opportunity for self-expression and self-awareness.

It is tempting to bypass the process of empathy when what we really seek is some change in our children's behavior or attitude. But remember, their behavior is based on feelings, and regardless of what they are feeling, that feeling is real to them. They may change their behavior to please us or to make life easier for the moment, but unless they have the opportunity to express what they're feeling and acknowledge it for what it is, they will have little understanding of why they feel the way they do and little motivation to make changes.

In trying to learn who they are, children are in the confusing early stages of a journey that will last a lifetime. The greater their self-awareness, the greater their confidence and their acceptance of others. Simply by providing your children with an open mind and an understanding heart, you are helping them know themselves.

In her thoughtful and realistic book about children's spiritual growth, *Something More,* Jean Grasso Fitzpatrick recounts the story of a father who was trying to persuade his two preschoolers to share a box of crayons. The four-year-old looked up at him and said plainly, "I don't like sharing!" The father, "about to say something like, 'Well, too bad!' " caught himself being honest, and answered, "You know, Catherine, neither do I." The girl looked startled, Fitzpatrick writes. "And then, of course, she shared the crayons." When she was able to confess her selfish feelings and find that they were normal, the child was able to take an unselfish action.

If we're honest with ourselves, we can identify with almost any feeling. But sharing a feeling does not mean we approve of an action. Feelings and actions are two different things. We have the license, the moral duty even, to make judgments about actions. But we do no good by placing judgments on another's feelings.

By acknowledging the difficulty of moral acts and admitting our contradictory feelings in that regard, we help our children make important moral choices. Just as important, we enable them, as Fitzpatrick puts it, to "confront their shortcomings in the knowledge that they are loved."

Respect

We show our respect for children by taking them seriously when they mean to be taken seriously. This is sometimes quite difficult. My three-year-old friend and I were playing with a balloon on a rubber band one day—bouncing each other on the head and giggling, over and over again. Suddenly she stopped playing and asked me in a slow, considered way, "Sara, why are you so silly?" It was apparent that she was serious. She was honestly trying to understand why a grownup was sitting on the floor playing with a balloon.

I answered, "I'm not always so silly. When I go to work, I'm not silly. But being silly is fun, and I like to have fun with you." She bounced the balloon off my head, and our silliness continued.

The same friend has also asked me very serious questions about death and God, and though I can offer her no easy answers on those matters, we talk about ideas and feelings that we are both trying to understand. Being able to talk makes us feel comfortable and close to each other.

One day, a group of my young friend's older relatives were teasing her about a simple but hilarious verbal mistake she had made. Later, she told her mother, "I don't want people to talk about that." The message was conveyed, and now we spare her the embarrassment.

At the age of three, this child knew she was entitled to respect. And she was also learning what it means to respect others. She called me a name one day, and I told her I didn't like it. "My momma lets me call my baby sister that name!"

she said. "OK," I said, "but I don't like for you to call me that. That name hurts my feelings." She patted me on the cheek and called me another silly name, one I didn't mind at all.

The author Robert Coles realized that all of his training as a child psychiatrist couldn't tell him who children were. He could learn everything adults had to say about children's physical and mental well-being, but children, like all of us, are more than the sum of those parts. To get to know children, Coles began listening to what they had to say about the important things in their lives. Many times, he started by asking them to draw pictures and talk about them.

In one Massachusetts fifth-grade classroom, he asked children to draw pictures that would "tell me, as best you can, who you are." The children drew, and then began discussing their drawings. The conversation turned quickly to God, prayer, and morality. One girl said, "We should do this more often."

Children, wrote Coles, "need no sanctification, but they do deserve a faithful accounting of what they said about themselves and their lives—the past as they remembered it, the present as they struggled to get through it, the future as they dreamt it might be. The longer I've known such children, the more readily I've noticed the abiding interest they have in reflecting about human nature, about the reasons people behave as they do, about the mysteries of the universe."

If we pay attention, we can easily see, like Coles, that "boys and girls are constantly at work noticing what is just, what is unjust, rendering their judgments." They are also at work thinking about God, marriage, money, jobs, friends, parents, and everything present and future that life might have in store.

Coles, in *The Moral Life of Children, The Political Life of Children,* and *The Spiritual Life of Children,* offered a glimpse of what takes place in children's hearts and minds. He listened, he took their words seriously, he asked them questions based not on his psychological analysis but simply on what they told him. In doing so, he encouraged them to think, to feel, and to come to a better understanding of themselves. And he learned that children are remarkably like us. "From early childhood until the last breath . . . we never stop trying to settle upon some satisfying idea of who and what we ourselves are."

When we are able to see our own hopes and strivings in a child, when we have empathy, we are better able to respect the child's journey.

Respect, like empathy, begins with paying attention. While empathy helps us recognize the similarities between our children and ourselves, respect helps us accept the differences between us. We demonstrate respect for our children's individuality when we allow them to dress the way they feel comfortable, to eat the foods they like, to listen to the music of their choice. Through respect, we give them the freedom to discover who they are, and help them become people who will foster the same freedom in others.

Acceptance

Parenting is great training for tolerance. Our children are quite different from us in ways we don't understand: they have different personalities, interests, abilities, tastes, and habits; they have different questions and dreams and fears for their lives; they wear strange clothes and hair styles, and listen to strange music. They have their own culture.

If we measure our parenting skills by how closely our children fit our expectations, we will surely be disappointed. Ironically, the more comfortable we are with ourselves, the less compelled we are to have our children look, think, talk, and act as we do.

The monk Thomas Merton wrote, "The beginning of love is to let those we love be perfectly themselves, and not to twist them to fit our own image. Otherwise we love only the reflection of ourselves we find in them."

Accepting, and enjoying, our differences will strengthen the bonds between ourselves and our children. In turn, we model for them a key skill of tolerance.

The novelist Robb Forman Dew wrote in *The Family Heart* about her personal struggle to accept her son Stephen's homosexuality. She had read all the "right" parenting books and worked hard to be a good mother. She had respected her children's individuality, even from birth.

Nineteen years later, she recognized with traumatic force how her expectations of her children were limited by society's prejudices and reinforced by the parenting "experts." Despite her early realization that Stephen was his own person, she had expected that he would, of course, be heterosexual. "So Stephen learned early to live his life in disguise."

Without the acceptance of their parents, gay children are left alone, to "grow up in a society that reflects back at them utter scorn for their legitimate emotions." Many of them choose not to live. The suicide rate for gays is at least three times the rate for heterosexuals.

Dew had, despite her best intentions, "failed to discern such a significant truth: that parents' assumptions of heterosexuality of their sons and daughters begin at birth and are a threat to their children's lives." She became involved with an organization called P-FLAG (Parents, Families, and Friends of Lesbians and Gays), which enabled her to be supportive and accepting of her son.

Wendy and Steve Northrup were also shocked to discover that, despite their best intentions, much of their parenting efforts were engineered to have their children fit a mold. The Northrups had worked hard to give their children all the moral guidance they could. They wrote, in *Helping Teens Care*, "We spent a lot of energy encouraging them to think of other people and to judge others by who they are, not by what they look like or where they live. We sent them to integrated schools to broaden their horizons and have them experience the gifts of other cultures and races . . . We had read all the right books and had tried hard to do all the right things."

But something was wrong. One daughter was anorexic, another was filled with an unidentifiable rage, and a son suddenly began failing in school. The family had therapy sessions, and "what our children screamed at us in those sessions, with anger we had never before experienced, was how much we expected of them and how conditioned our love was on their fulfilling those expectations."

The Northrups' son reminded them of the time he wanted to give up swimming and take up skateboarding. His parents told him he could choose his own goals in life, but they let him know how disappointed they were in his choice.

Awakened by her children's criticism, Wendy Northrup remembered an incident that took place on a family trip to Disney World. While all her children were enjoying the Jungle Ride in the Magic Kingdom, she took the opportunity to "begin a lecture on the stereotypes of native people that we encountered." The children cried in frustration, "Mom! Can't we just enjoy this for a change?"

"They were right," Wendy Northrup would later write. "They had no chance to find their own way, to explore their own values, because mine were always there, challenging them at every turn."

It was only after the Northrups took a close look at themselves that they were able to accept their children. "Perhaps the hardest lesson for us to learn has been to accept the children unconditionally and love them for themselves, not for the way they reflect our values and dreams," they wrote. "We have always known this lesson. We even recognized blatant violations of it in other parents . . . But until we looked very carefully, we had no idea how conditioned our love appeared to them."

What Wendy and Steve Northrup finally recognized was "how bound we were to others' opinions and how much our actions were motivated by the expectations of others. We didn't really trust ourselves to do the right thing without outside pressures, and we transferred that lack of trust to our children."

For years, Wendy had lived with the fear that "I wouldn't be good enough and that my children wouldn't be good enough." Recognizing that fear, and the influence it had in her life, enabled her to release it. She was able at last to accept herself. "Believing in ourselves," she wrote, "gave us the freedom to believe in our children."

The crisis of her daughter's anorexia taught her something else about acceptance: sometimes it means letting go. "One of the first, and perhaps the most important, insights has been that the only people we can change are ourselves." And when Wendy and Steve quit taking responsibility for their daughter's illness, the girl chose to take on the responsibility herself and began a program of recovery.

Confronted with crisis in the family, the Northrups were able to face themselves and begin to change. They let go of the control they had tried to exercise over their children's lives, and they got to work on themselves. In the end, they wrote, "At this moment we believe that the greatest gift we can give our children is to model for them that we can face hard things about ourselves and lovingly do something about them together."

Forgiveness

Forgiveness is love in the midst of disappointment. When we are let down by someone we love, we want most of all to let them know how hurt we are. And that's all right. We should. But if we want to let go of the pain we feel, our only alternative is forgiveness.

Forgiveness is easier when apologies are offered, when we understand the reasons behind the offense, when the wrong was unintended, and when we want to preserve the relationship. But even when none of these things is true, when the offense is hateful, purposeful, and when we have no interest in maintaining a relationship with the offender, forgiveness is necessary—not for the offender's sake, but for ours.

Forgiveness is something we do for ourselves. If we can't forgive, we are left with resentments and anger, and we will not be happy. Just as acceptance means letting go of control, forgiveness means letting go of pain. In families, forgiveness enables us to continue our lives together without being trapped in resentment and distrust.

Forgiveness is not called for unless some wrong is done. Our children don't need our forgiveness for anything they feel or are—these are not wrong. They do need our forgiveness, as much as they need our guidance, when they've done harm, broken rules, or made mistakes.

The first step in forgiveness is to acknowledge the harm that was done. If you make fun of me, I must admit that I am embarrassed and hurt before I can forgive you. If you lie to me, I must admit I feel used and betrayed before I can forgive you. When we cannot own up to our hurt feelings, we are likely to respond with anger instead of honesty, with punishment instead of forgiveness.

When we express our hurt or anger in acts of retribution, we lay the groundwork for shame, a most unhealthy feeling. When we are able to tell our children what we feel in response to their violations, we offer them the chance to feel guilty—a healthy response to wrongdoing. And when we forgive them, we let them know that they can make mistakes without losing our love. When they know this, they are better able to face their own failures, accept their imperfections, and forgive the failures of others.

Just as important as our ability to forgive our children is the ability to forgive ourselves. Maya Angelou tells about a conversation she was having with a white friend when the man made the unconscious verbal distinction between "black boys" and "our boys" in discussing American soldiers at war. His shame was such that he avoided talking to Angelou for a long while afterward. Only when he forgave himself did he overcome the rift and renew his friendship with Angelou, who had forgiven him long ago.

In the same way, our own guilt and shame can paralyze our relationships with those we love. Not until we can forgive ourselves the harm we've done as parents are we ever completely free to enjoy our families.

At times, too, we have to ask for forgiveness. This is tough. There are two sentences, it seems, that we humans have great difficulty speaking: "I don't know" and "I was wrong." It takes some practice, being able to say these words. But once we've said "I was wrong" a few times, we find it really isn't such a terrible thing to be wrong. People are wrong all the time. Why should we expect ourselves to be any different?

It can be especially hard for parents to admit their mistakes. After all, what will happen to our children's respect for our authority, their trust in our decisions, if we admit we're wrong?

The truth is, healthy children generally aren't true believers in their parents' perfection anyway. If they have learned to trust their own judgments, they will know when we are wrong without our saying so. By admitting it, we tell them that in addition to being sometimes wrong, we are also mostly honest.

A woman who was having trouble with her husband took her anger out on her children, ages four and six. She was impatient when they needed something, she never stopped to play with them, and when they wanted to talk to her she put them off with words and gestures. After she talked with a counselor and released the anger she felt, it dawned on her that her treatment of the children was unfair, that it was a reflection of the rage she had built up toward her husband.

The next time she found herself snapping at one of the children, she gathered them both to her side and asked, "Do you feel as if Mommy doesn't like you?" "Yes!" they answered together. "I was afraid of that," she said. "I've been ignoring you and I've been impatient and I haven't been fair.

But that's my problem. It's not your fault. I love you very much and I'm sorry." The children's relief was palpable, and so was the mother's. Not only did the children forgive her instantly, they became less desperate for her attention once they knew they still had her love.

Learning to ask for forgiveness and taking the opportunity to forgive are among the most valuable lessons in human relationships. Mark Honeywell Summit describes, in *Helping Teens Care,* an incident of his father striking his brother in the face. "After a few minutes to cool off, my father took the initiative to go to my brother's room to apologize, to begin the process of reconciliation. There were wounds that needed to be healed, and he knew it was necessary to do his part in that healing process . . . These lessons of reconciliation have been valuable for me and have been necessary ones to bring to relationships I have developed since then. The tools of reconciliation are a gift I received from my family, especially my parents."

Involvement

We will never be as important to another human being as we are to a newborn baby. In all cultures, healthy children are those who have had a steady caregiver, there for them at all times. It doesn't have to be the mother, and in many cases it's not, but it has to be someone.

For obvious reasons, social scientists haven't tried to conduct experiments to determine what happens when human babies are systematically left alone. But we know from the anecdotal evidence that babies who are consistently ignored become children likely to be insecure, fearful, distrustful, or angry. The same is true in primate families, observed Melvin Konner. Baby monkeys separated from their mothers "may grow up with severe, even grotesque behavioral abnormalities, such as . . . self-biting, hyperaggressiveness . . . and even abusive parenting."

Researchers are finally coming to the consensus that abundant love does not spoil a baby. Infants need to learn first and foremost that they belong, and that someone will be there for them, before they can develop confidence and self-discipline.

As our children develop bonds outside the family, their dependence on us lessens. But their need for our involvement, our attention, remains. Children need us to be a part of their lives *all* their lives.

If our relationship to our children is based on empathy, acceptance, and respect, our involvement in their lives comes more easily. We can be comfortable in one another's company because there is an established emotional bond. We can be curious about each other's thoughts and feelings because we know we don't have to agree with them and we aren't responsible for them. We can admire their interests and skills because we have accepted their distinct individuality as well as our own. We can simply have fun together because we feel free to be ourselves.

We all have, at one time or another, experienced judgment and criticism from a parent in the form of emotional withdrawal. Taken to extremes, withdrawal can turn into long-term estrangement, not only between teenagers and parents, but between adult children and parents.

Involvement with our children's lives allows us the opportunity to know them without trying to change who they are; it gives them the opportunity to know us, in all our strengths and weaknesses; and not insignificantly, it restores to us some of the wonder of childhood that we still need.

I was carrying a two-year-old friend down the driveway one night when we both saw a brilliant full moon come out from behind the trees. "Ooooh!" I said. "Ooooh!" she said. "That's *my* moon," she said. "Would you share it with me?" I asked. "Yes," she said. It was a stunning moment of ordinary beauty, and I could think of no one better to share it with than a two-year-old.

Children give us a chance to be childlike in its best senses. We can, without self-consciousness, experience wonder, joy, and pure silliness. We can ask questions there are no answers to. We can hug and sing and jump and shout. We can play. And we can build a habit of interest in our children's lives that can sustain us even through the difficult times when our children don't seem very interested in us.

The theologian Henri J. M. Nouwen describes the relationship between parents and children in terms of hospitality—hospitality meaning "the creation of a free space where the stranger can enter and become a friend instead of an enemy." Children, he writes, "are not properties to own and rule over, but gifts to cherish and care for. Our children are our most important guests, who enter into our home, ask for careful attention, stay for a while and then leave to follow their own way. Children are strangers whom we have to get to know. They have their own style, their own rhythm, and their own capacities for good and evil. They cannot be explained by looking at their parents."

We should be grateful, Nouwen suggests, that our children are not ours to train "as a lion tamer trains his lions. They are guests we have to respond to, not possessions we are responsible for."

When we become empathic, accepting, respectful, and forgiving participants in our children's lives, we display the skills of tolerance, and we offer them a place of safety and belonging where they know they are loved. There is no better preparation for tolerance than this.

Still, to become tolerant, our children need more than love—they need help. Our youngest especially, because they are just learning how to be in the world, need guidance to care for themselves and for others. If we love them and show them how tolerance works in our own lives, they are well on their way. But we can also help them by providing a background of moral knowledge, guidelines for moral behavior, and opportunities to make moral choices.

〜

JOURNAL NOTES
CHAPTER 5

1. **Empathy.** The technique Vivian Paley used to understand her kindergartners is based on two simple steps: "finding the child and recording the story." By "finding the child," she means finding in herself the same feelings her children express. By "recording the story," she means writing down "discoveries, anecdotes, questions, memories, and doubts." She says, "There is, I think, no other way to keep track of the elusive self, ours or the children's."

Describe an incident involving your child that was confusing or frustrating for you. Record how the child looked, what she said and did. What feelings did she express? How did you react? Put yourself in your child's place. Try to recall a similar problem in your own life, as a child or an adult. What were your feelings? How did you deal with them?

2. **Respect.** Recall a time in your childhood when you felt humiliated by an adult. Describe the circumstances and the feelings you had.

3. **Acceptance.** Did your parents ever try to change something about you? Describe the circumstances. How did you feel? What do you imagine your parents were feeling?

Have you ever been embarrassed by something about

your child? What did you feel like doing? What did you say or do? Why might you have had those feelings and that reaction?

4. **Forgiveness.** Remember a resentment you held against a parent, child, or spouse. Describe the incident. What happened and how did you feel? What problems resulted from your resentment? Of what benefit was your resentment? Write down what you would like to say to the other person, expressing your feelings as honestly as you can, and end with a statement of forgiveness.

5. **Involvement.** Write about a time when you were interested in some activity that your parents did not understand or appreciate. What message did you receive about yourself and about your interests from that experience? What effect did their lack of interest have on your relationship with them? How did you feel about yourself?

Directions
for the Journey

Many things must happen, many things
must go right, a whole constellation of
events must be fulfilled, for one human
being to successfully advise or help
another.
RAINER MARIA RILKE

A white couple who wanted their five-year-old to learn the value of diversity enrolled him in an integrated kindergarten. On his third day of school, Tommy came home in angry tears; he'd had a fight over a toy with a boy named Michael. Knowing that Michael was African American, Tommy's worried mother asked if he liked other children who looked like Michael. Tommy rolled his eyes and sighed as if she had just asked the stupidest question in the world. "Mo-omm, I know!" he said. "Brown people are nice nice nice nice *NICE!*"

At five, Tommy had already learned what he was supposed to think about brown people, but that had little relevance to the problem he was having with one brown boy in particular. He was fortunate to have a mother who was willing to learn from him. Tommy's mom heard the frustration and anger in his "brown people are nice" response, and she immediately empathized. Just because he was learning that all people are equal didn't mean that he was going to get along with all people equally well. In all the stories she had read to him, where people of different colors, religions, and cultures live together in harmony, she had failed to mention that it was sometimes just as difficult to get along with brown people as it was to get along with white ones. Now he was finding that out on his own, and he simply didn't know what to do.

Tommy's mom understood that what he needed now was not another empty generalization, but some realistic guidance in learning how to think about his problem, how to cope with his feelings, and how to control his own actions. Together, Tommy and his mother talked about a plan of action. It would take several weeks, but eventually Tommy and Michael found ways to play together peacefully.

Learning how to get along with others is a complicated internal process that takes place in our minds and our hearts as well as in our actions. We know what tolerance is, we have a desire to become tolerant, and we learn to practice tolerance. And it doesn't happen all at once. Like Tommy, we know it's right to be fair, but our feelings sometimes fly in the face of what we know.

Tommy's mom, like all moms, would have liked to offer him a word or a touch to make him feel better, think more clearly, and act nicer instantaneously. But becoming tolerant is always a journey. We cannot carry our children through it, but, having made the journey ourselves, we can offer directions. Whether or not they choose to follow them is beyond our control. We are their loving guardians, not their gods. And that's as it should be. They would never become complete individuals if it were otherwise.

One thing we've learned from our own inventory is that our ability to express tolerance depends largely on cognitive and emotional processes that are sometimes hidden from us. It's easier to change our behavior when we are aware of what we think and how we feel. This chapter and the next will focus on helping children tap inner sources of tolerance— habits of thought and feeling that help us respect differences and diminish barriers between us. Chapter 8 will focus on helping children practice the outer expressions of tolerance.

Moral Messages

The most important cognitive tools we can give our children are a store of moral knowledge and invitations to think for themselves.

Most of our moral knowledge is rooted in the spiritual traditions of the world's faiths, but it isn't necessary for us to pray to the same God, go to the same church, or go to any church at all to be part of the unity of moral wisdom. What's important for our children to learn is that human beings in all cultures have certain ideas about how we ought to live together. We don't always follow the codes of behavior that we believe in, but we must continue to try.

James Q. Wilson, in *The Moral Sense,* argues that the notion of morality is universal. "What is remarkable—indeed, what constitutes the most astonishing thing about the moral development of humanity—has been the slow, uneven, but more or less steady expansion of the idea that the moral sense ought to govern a wide range—perhaps, indeed, the whole range—of human interactions."

By teaching our children the principles that most human beings agree on, we give them a set of ideals to strive for in their relationships with others. We know that these principles cannot be perfectly achieved, and that we ourselves, along with many people we encounter, will often violate them, both by mistake and by intention. But the ideals we share are of vital importance nevertheless. They help guide us when we are confused; they help us discover where we have been wrong; they give us goals to aim for; and they offer hope that change is possible. Most important, they comfort us in the knowledge that, no matter how unpredictable and chaotic our world seems, there is a source of universal principles available to us all.

Among those principles are:

1. All people are valuable. No one is better than anyone else.
2. No one is perfect. We all make mistakes.
3. In some ways, we are just like everyone else on Earth. We all share the same feelings.
4. In some ways, we are different from everyone else on Earth. Each of us has a unique personality and appearance.
5. All people—no matter who they are, where they come from, what they believe, how they act, or what they look like—deserve respect and compassion.
6. Each of us is responsible for our own actions.
7. To be happy and secure, we need other people in our lives.
8. We should treat other people the way we want others to treat us.

As difficult as they are to live by, most of these ideals can be stated quite simply. We find them in proverbs, in the traditions of our cultures, and in the world's religious faiths. We remind ourselves of them by telling stories, repeating poems, singing songs, saying prayers, recounting legends, and reading literature. When we articulate these truths in the simple phrases that we have learned from our families, we offer our children a language for the inner voice of conscience, an unchanging source of wisdom that they can rely on when the temptations of intolerance arise.

When we help our children see the connections between these principles and everyday events, we offer them simple moral memories that they can call upon again and again for guidance.

Sometimes, knowing what is right and what is wrong is the only comfort we have from cruelty. When I was in elementary school, the standard slur used for anyone who fumbled a ball, tripped on the stairs, or didn't know the answer to a question, was "*re*-tard." My younger brother was retarded, and I loved him. Whenever I heard the word, accented heavily on the first syllable, I stiffened myself against an onslaught of hurt and embarrassment, and felt immediately and irretrievably isolated from the speakers. I understood from their words that other people, some of them my own friends, looked down on my brother and those like him as if they were lesser beings. There was nothing I could do or say to ease my disappointment in their meanness. But I knew they were wrong. The children's insults hurt, but they did not alter me. I was sure of what I believed and whom I loved, and in that certainty was a kind of comfort.

Independent Thinking

By repeating the values we hold dear, we offer our children security in the knowledge that some things are unquestionably true, that people really do know how to live together in peace, and that the ones closest to them have strong values and convictions. In a world that's so often contradictory and confusing, our children need to be shown and told over and over again that some things are simply right and some are simply wrong.

But memorizing a litany of *do's* and *don'ts* is not enough. Our ideals are general principles that contain our vision of ourselves and our world at its best. They are not panaceas for every circumstance of life. If our children are to live with values of tolerance, they must learn to think for themselves.

We are all born with certain patterns of thinking that promote intolerance, as shown in Chapter 3. To make sense of the world, we categorize, draw quick conclusions, rank people and things, conform to others' thinking, and prefer the familiar. These are universal human traits that are necessary and often helpful. But they need to be balanced with the skills of independent thinking—the cognitive habits that help us take a closer look at the world and at ourselves.

People who are tolerant tend to have realistic, flexible styles of thinking. That is, they are not disturbed by ambiguity or uncertainty; they appreciate the mysteries of life. They greet new information and new people with curiosity rather than fear; they are creative and imaginative thinkers. They can accurately discern another person's point of view; they are comfortable when saying "I don't know," and they aren't compelled to fix blame when things go wrong.

The most important influence on a person's thinking style may not be specific instruction but the freedom and security that come from growing up in a loving home. Parents who are comfortable with themselves and others tend to raise children who are free to explore their own imaginations, to look at things from many perspectives, and to wait for evidence rather than jump to conclusions. Such children have learned to ask questions, and they have also learned that not all questions have answers. They understand both that they can make their own judgments and that they are responsible for the judgments they make.

Children learn these thinking skills best when they witness them in the lives of the people they love, and when they have abundant opportunities to practice them. These are a few of the most basic independent thinking skills that we can practice in our lives and encourage in our children.

· *There is more than one way to look at anything.*

The moonshadows on a bedroom wall turn into monsters. The stuffed tiger becomes a best friend. Pots and pans are drums to bang on, hats to wear, or boats to drive. Young children are blessed with limitless imaginations that allow them to see the world in many different ways. As they grow and the pressure builds to conform to others' ways of thinking, children start to put away the tools of imagination. The world becomes something to figure out rather than something to wonder about. It is more important to be right than to have fun. The urge to draw conclusions grows strong. And it becomes a habit to settle on one way of looking at things, shutting out the alternatives, closing our minds.

In Victorian England, the wolf was a symbol of evil, a vicious enemy of man that would kill unless killed first. Old legends and contemporary horror stories fueled the terror that accompanied any sighting of a wolf. The werewolf entered the popular imagination as a symbol of humanity possessed by evil forces.

At the same time, the Indians of North America, far less educated by European standards, had a vastly different view of the wolf. For them, the wolf was an animal to be honored, a symbol of strength and courage and loyalty. To align oneself with the spirit of the wolf was to become a person of great integrity. So wolves in North America were respected and avoided, and wolves in Europe were hunted and killed.

When Europeans settled North America, of course, they also viewed the Indians as savages, and they set about trying to rid their new communities of wolves and Indians alike. Within a few generations, most Indians had been killed or confined to far-off reservations, and the population of North American wolves was near extinction. It did not occur to the Europeans that white people, wolves, and Indians might all find a way to live together peacefully. They found it easier to alter their world than to change their minds.

Changing our minds requires a great deal of intellectual courage. To acknowledge that our way of seeing is not the only way requires a strong sense of personal security. Children who are just learning to make judgments about the world around them are full of mistaken ideas about people and things. Their ability to generalize from limited information naturally surpass their ability to withhold judgment or to re-evaluate their assumptions. New information is unsettling and sometimes threatening.

We can help children become open-minded by demon-strating curiosity in the face of the unfamiliar, by asserting our belief that there is always something more to learn, and by sharing with them how our own ideas and attitudes have changed with time. Most important, we can remind our children of our love and respect for them even when they make mistakes. Learning is about making mistakes, we can tell them, and true wisdom is being able to admit when we're wrong: When we work a new jigsaw puzzle, we are often wrong about what piece goes where. It's not until we abandon our old ideas and try out new ones that we learn how all the pieces fit.

Once we accept that there are many different ways to look at things, and that it's OK to make mistakes, we have the gift of intellectual freedom: we can be curious about all the world, and we don't have to fear the unfamiliar. We understand that just because something seems odd doesn't mean it's wrong. One of Dr. Seuss's classics, *Green Eggs and Ham,* teaches just that. The stubborn resistor, who is com-pelled to claim his name each time he unleashes his preju-dice against green eggs and ham, finally cannot resist the call of the imagination, and he summons the courage to try something he has judged to be utterly repulsive. He finds out to his great joy that he does, in fact, like green eggs and ham, and maybe he's learned that being open-minded can lead to all kinds of exciting adventures.

As simple as Dr. Seuss's lesson sounds, we adults have a terrible time following it. Almost without realizing it, we develop fixed ideas, just as we have certain ways of doing things, and any variation on those ideas disrupts our equilibrium.

· *We can learn and grow by listening to others.*

One of our hardest tasks is to pay attention to each other. Only when our interest in someone else surpasses our interest in ourselves do we set aside our own thoughts and open ourselves to the thoughts of other people.

Listening attentively, because it interferes with our natural self-centeredness, takes practice. Most of our mental energies are focused on ourselves—on what we want, what we think, and what we feel. When someone else is talking to us, we typically spend our time thinking about how we will respond and waiting for that interval when we can speak. The more insecure we are, the greater our compulsion to make our case, to defend our concepts of the world and ourselves. We can listen only when we are not threatened by new ideas, when we feel comfortable with uncertainty and ambiguity, and when we understand that, by listening, we give ourselves an opportunity to grow and learn.

To listen with attention, we have to think differently from the way we are accustomed. We have to free our minds to the words being offered; we have to expect that, by listening, we will learn something. There are guidelines for listening well that we can practice and help our children practice.

1. When someone is talking to you, give her your attention. Rather than fighting her ideas with your own arguments, or trying to think of something to

add, simply listen for the meaning of the other person's words. Instead of asking yourself, "What can I say next?" ask yourself, "What is she saying now?"

2. Don't interrupt while another person is speaking. When we interrupt, we are telling the other person that we don't care what she has to say.

3. Allow yourself to be curious about what the other person is saying. Ask questions. Engage in a quest for clarity. We usually don't express ourselves perfectly or completely, and we need the help of another person asking us questions, rephrasing our words, and allowing us the opportunity to explain and revise our ideas.

4. Try to identify with the message you're hearing. We know we have understood somebody when we can "feel" what she is talking about. Even when we strongly disagree with someone's thoughts, we can often hear behind the words some feeling that we have shared.

When we learn to listen carefully to another person, focusing on the things we share rather than the things we disagree with, we become more comfortable with points of view that are different from our own, and we become open to greater learning. But listening well doesn't give us license to abandon our own judgments. In the end, only we are responsible for what we think.

- *No one has all the answers.*

One of the great handicaps suffered by prejudiced people is the tendency to believe that those in authority are unequivocally right, and that there is an answer for everything. "Highly prejudiced children," wrote Gordon Allport, tend to believe that "there is only one right way to do anything." Out of their "longing for definiteness, for safety, for authority" comes a "constrictedness in thinking . . . Where there is no order they impose it. When new solutions are called for they cling to tried and tested habits. Wherever possible they latch onto what is familiar, safe, simple, definite."

The link between prejudice and a love for authority is so strong that sociologists have found that their measures of the authoritarian personality also describe people who are prejudiced. People who match these descriptions were often raised to see their parents as absolute rulers and themselves as obedient subjects who dared not question or challenge the wisdom of their superiors. Children naturally long for certainty, but a strict authoritarian environment provides them with absolutes that are intellectually and emotionally debilitating.

Children should know that no one, not even Father or Mother, always knows best, that sometimes even when we think we know, we're wrong, and that there are some things nobody knows.

Part of our job as parents is to protect the mysteries of the world. As much as our children might like us to be all-knowing, they need to hear us say things like: "I wonder why . . ." "What do you think about . . . ?" "What would happen if . . . ?" "Do you suppose . . . ?"

Children are full of questions: "How does the car go?" "Are there people on other planets?" "Why do we change the clocks for summertime?" We can see in all their questions an opportunity to encourage curiosity and creativity, and to let them know that much of life is still a mystery, even to grownups.

Instead of trying to answer all their questions, one teacher has children explain, in as many different ways as they can, why zebras have stripes, for instance, or what the dark side of the moon looks like. Their answers, while they may be "wrong," are inventive and thoughtful. By encouraging their sense of wonder, we help children practice the learning power of questions and explore the mystery of what we don't know.

· *We must make our own judgments and decisions. And we are responsible for the decisions we make.*

Ultimately, the way we learn what's true is not by accepting what's told to us, but by asking questions, raising doubts, testing our theories by experience, and scrutinizing an idea from a variety of positions.

Young children, whose reasoning powers are limited, form judgments from firsthand experience, but have a tendency to generalize wildly. The only way to convince them otherwise is to give them new experiences.

In a rural Southern town, a five-year-old boy refused to

let a girl play with his toy planes. When his kindergarten teacher asked him why, he insisted, "Girls can't drive airplanes." It took some searching, but a couple of days later the teacher found some books with photographs of women pilots and astronauts to show the class.

Many of children's mistaken views about race have more to do with their thinking skills than with their racial attitudes. Patricia Ramsey, in Carolyn Pope Edwards' *Promoting Social and Moral Development in Young Children*, describes the evolution of children's racial thinking as a mysterious but oddly consistent process that begins with the assumption that skin color is not permanent.

"I wish those white kids would hurry up and get their suntans so that they'd be nice and brown like me," said four-year-old Althea in one classroom.

James, four and a half, said of a black classmate who was washing her hands at the sink, "She's gonna have to wash her hands real hard to get all that brown off."

"I think the doctor dyed me brown," said Jerry, not quite five. When the teacher asked, "Could you change that?" Jerry said, "Yeah, but I'd have to really pull my skin off like this"—tugs at his skin—"and the blood might spill out."

Ramsey describes one teacher who sought to challenge the children's thinking about skin colors by washing a black doll to demonstrate that skin color was permanent. The children's observations were predictable, depending on their age. The three-year-olds imagined they could see the black doll's skin growing lighter; the four-year-olds were puzzled that the doll's color didn't change, but they expected it would eventually; and the five-year-olds had no patience for the exercise. The black doll was "supposed to be that way," said one of them. Children's thinking skills develop at their own pace. We can offer them evidence and answers, but they have to be ready to accept them.

With older children, teachers use "critical thinking" exercises to encourage the habits of questioning, re-evaluating, and making informed judgments. Critical thinking skills help us separate fact from opinion and ideas from feelings. We learn that we can disagree with each other without anger or loss of respect.

In one class, the topic of gun control is brought up for debate. Students in favor of gun control are asked to make the best argument they can for opposing it, and students opposed to gun control are asked to prepare an argument in favor of it. The point is not to change the students' minds, but to challenge them to take their opponents' views seriously, and to examine the basis of their own views. In so doing, the students learn that there are valid arguments on both sides, and that just because another person holds a different view does not make that person wrong or ignorant.

Critical thinking requires the steady attention and patience that are necessary, for example, when examining an optical illusion. It means assuming there is something more to the picture than is first apparent. Above all, it means seeking the truth.

People who have learned to think critically can distinguish between eloquent deception and plain truth. The impact of an argument is in the soundness of its reasoning, not in the force with which it is argued. Exaggeration and generalization are useless devices. The whole purpose of learning, reasoning, and making judgments is to come closer to the truth, not to claim victory for one's opinions.

It's easy, even for the most astute minds, to abandon the elements of critical thinking when it comes to personal relationships. Whenever we use all-inclusive terms, such as "they," "always," and "never," or express our opinions about people in broad generalizations, we not only discredit our argument, but we exercise an unearned license to judge people categorically, and we model the practice of stereotyping.

When children are encouraged to investigate the evidence before making judgments, when their broad categorizations are challenged, when they are allowed to make up their own minds without coercion or condescension, they come to trust their own ability to make decisions. And they also learn that those decisions are their responsibility. No one else has imposed them and no one else can change them.

All these habits of tolerant thinking are more than mere intellectual exercises. They require a sense of personal security that tells us we are more than what we think. Children who grow up knowing they are loved for who they are, not for what they achieve or what they believe, can more easily cope with cognitive confusion, uncertainty, differences, and contradictions. It seems true that we cannot become open-minded unless we also learn to open our hearts.

〜

JOURNAL NOTES
CHAPTER 6

1. **Moral messages.** What are some of the sayings you recall from your childhood that helped define your values? What other sources of moral messages did you have?

2. **Democratic principles.** Look at the eight principles listed on page 111. They are assertions of human equality, fallibility, similarity, individuality, integrity, responsibility, interdependence, and empathy. Which of these principles did you understand early in your life? How did you learn them? Which of these principles were not part of your upbringing? What messages did you receive that may have conflicted with any of these principles?

3. **Listening.** Review the listening guidelines on pages 117–18. Rate yourself as a listener according to whether you always, often, occasionally, or never practice these habits.

4. **Independent thinking.** When you and your children disagree, what is your first reaction: to convince them you

are right, to ignore the disagreement, to explore the reasons
for their opinions, to condemn or ridicule their viewpoint?

5. Conflict. Describe your feelings when you discover
that someone you care about deeply disagrees with you
about something that is very important to you.

CHAPTER 7

The Heart
of Tolerance

We are more alike, my friend,
than we are unalike.
MAYA ANGELOU

Carlos, who has just turned five, is playing with his new
sword in the living room, swiping fiercely at an imaginary
foe and shouting, "Hi-yah!" with every thrust. His sister,
three, watches in awe for a few moments, then asks whether
she can play with the sword. Carlos ignores her until she
tries to take the sword away.

"No, Lena!" he says in exasperation. "It's not for girls."

At five, Carlos has already learned so much. He has
learned, even if subconsciously, that a certain moral order
exists in opposition to his own selfish desires. It's no longer
acceptable for him to get what he wants just because he

wants it. "No! Mine!" is not good enough. He knows he is expected to share and to consider other people's needs. And while he is not willing, in this case, to act on the principle of sharing, he does not wish to be seen as violating that principle. So he has to invent a rationale for his selfishness that appears, to his mind, to make sense.

The solution he comes up with ("It's not for girls") is brilliant. In one stroke, it accommodates his own love of certainty, his passion for rules, his skills at generalizing and categorization, and his need to control the situation and protect his self-interest. The only problem with his reasoning is that he can't get away with it.

In fact, Carlos's reaction shocks his father, who has consciously sought to avoid the kind of gender stereotypes he grew up with. "Carlos, girls can play with swords, too," he says firmly. "Let Lena have a turn."

In Carlos's limited experience, Dad seems wrong. The television commercial that advertised this sword showed not a single girl playing with it. The pictures on the toy package showed no girls. And in his own experience, he has never seen a girl with a sword.

The world has offered him the perfect justification for keeping his sword, but Dad won't buy it. Carlos is outraged. He tries for a while to pretend he doesn't hear Dad's order. When that becomes impossible, he throws the sword down on the living room floor, calls the sword and everyone there "stupid," and stomps out.

Carlos is not conscious, just as we are often not conscious, of the mental calculations he has gone through to try to get his way. The moral impulse that requires him to justify his actions also helps him hide his real motivations from himself. Because he understands it isn't right to be selfish, he has difficulty even acknowledging that he feels that way. So he rationalizes his selfishness as being only reasonable. When his rationalization fails to get him what he wants and he becomes angry, it is righteous anger: he is right; they are wrong.

For Carlos to change his attitude about girls and swords, he will have to admit his own feelings, beginning with selfishness. That's an unlikely prospect for a five-year-old, but he has already begun the process. He has felt and expressed his anger. And next time, Carlos will have a new rule to work with: he must share his toys—even his sword, even with girls. The rule will help him behave appropriately, and as he changes his behavior, his heart and mind may also change. He may discover that it doesn't feel so bad to share. Girls may make good swashbucklers, after all.

The techniques of tolerance are so difficult not because they command a superior intelligence, but because they require a certain degree of emotional equanimity. The lessons Carlos has in store for him are among the hardest lessons to learn: that we aren't always right, that we can't always have our way, that we are not better than any other person, and that sometimes we need to act in ways we don't want to.

Research has clearly shown that the attitudes and behaviors associated with prejudice are often rooted in fear, insecurity, frustration, and anger—feelings that we all have from time to time. Not until we recognize our feelings can we sort out our thoughts, separating our valid judgments from rationalizations, and begin developing the habits of tolerance.

The complexities of our mental and emotional entanglements are mind-boggling. Fortunately, we come to know our own hearts not by analyzing the complexities, but by being, simply, ourselves; by honestly admitting our feelings and responsibly expressing them. When we learn from this process, we find that the old tricks of intolerant thinking are no longer useful. We can't disguise ourselves from ourselves by focusing on the faults of others. This is a long and difficult process that is made easier when the people around us accept us and encourage us to express emotions.

Feelings Check

When we learn to identify and express what we feel, we don't have to be trapped in our feelings. We gain a measure of security in the midst of any crisis by knowing that our feelings are not wrong, that they don't control us, and that they won't last forever. The insecurity and the self-deception of the prejudiced person leave little freedom for self-expression and no escape from the feelings of fear and inadequacy that can isolate us from others. By learning to express, accept, and let go of our negative feelings, we become more content with ourselves and more accepting of others.

As parents, we sometimes find it difficult to let our children simply feel their feelings, because so frequently we would like to change them. We see the children sad and want to make them happy; we see them angry and want to make them calm; we see them hostile and want to make them loving; we see them timid and we want to make them confident.

It's important for us to realize, and for our children to learn, that feelings are changed only from the inside. We can comfort our children, love them through their pain, and offer them ways to express themselves, but we can't take away their feelings.

Even though we can do little to alter our children's feelings, we can talk about and model for them our own understanding of what it means to acknowledge a problem and take responsibility for our feelings about that situation. Following are some of the insights we can communicate to them.

· *Feelings are not right or wrong. They're real.*

Children need us to affirm their right to their own feelings, even when they express those feelings in inappropriate ways. "It's OK to be angry, but it's not OK to throw things in the house." Or, "Sometimes we are surprised and afraid when we see people whose bodies look very different from ours. That's normal at first. But we have to remember that all people, no matter what they look like, are like us on the inside, and they deserve caring and respect. So we shouldn't stare at them or call them names."

Just as they need an open invitation to talk about their feelings, children also have the right to keep their feelings private. Most of all, they need us to accept the truth about their feelings. Feelings may disguise other feelings, and sometimes we don't know how to say what we feel. Crying, for instance, may be a sign of sadness, frustration, anger, fear, pain, pity, or even joy. Sometimes we hurt and don't know why. Admitting our confusion about our feelings is a first step toward self-acceptance.

· *Since our feelings are part of us, only we are responsible for them.*

We tend to assume that whatever we are feeling is the result of something real that has happened to us, and can be fixed only by a change in something outside ourselves. We feel jealousy when we're afraid of not being loved enough, whether or not there is any real evidence to support our fears. We feel rejected when we are left off a party list, whether or not rejection was intended. We feel humiliated when we are called an ugly name, even though there is no truth in what was said about us.

Among children's greatest fears, along with fear of the dark and fear of abandonment, is the fear of being ridiculed. It is almost impossible for them not to respond with intense embarrassment at being teased. The only consolation in such circumstances may be the idea that "just because they say it doesn't make it so." We are not responsible for what people say about us; we are responsible only for who we are.

Julia, a seven-year-old African American, came home from school one day and told her mother, "I wish I weren't brown." Nancy, her mother, recalls in Peggy Gillespie's

√*Other: Portraits of Multiracial Families,* "She spilled out a story about a little girl calling her names at school quite a while before. Julia had internalized it because she didn't have any handle to understand what had happened. Right away, I said, 'Julia, there's no problem with you. The problem is with this girl and I feel sorry for a girl who talks to people this way. It's *her problem.*' After hearing my explanation, Julia really changed. She realized that it was fine to be just the way she was." The girl who had teased Julia apologized, and Julia was able to forgive her. They became friends.

Our feelings may emerge in response to circumstances outside us, but they are not created by those circumstances. They are formed in our hearts. If we want to achieve self-acceptance and peace with others, we must take responsibility for what we feel. This is, for adults as well as children, one of the more difficult tasks of growing up. It means being able to accept on a deep level that only we, and no one else, can change the way we feel.

· *It's important to identify our feelings, whether we are comfortable with them or not.*

If we can't identify a reason for our feelings, we often try to hide those feelings completely. "I've got a great job and wonderful coworkers. I can't be unhappy here." Every time we bury a feeling, we become a prisoner to it. Only by admitting our feelings can we get past them.

Research has found that prejudiced people judge themselves especially harshly for any negative feelings they may have about themselves or their families. Loneliness, anger, hate, jealousy, resentment—they have become so afraid of admitting these feelings that they go to great lengths, including projecting them outward as prejudices, in order to create an illusion of a secure existence. Yet their lives are ruled by the feelings they can't face up to.

Tolerant people, on the other hand, usually have little problem expressing mixed feelings about their upbringing; there were good days and bad days, and their parents weren't perfect. By acknowledging the pain, they can keep it in a healthy perspective.

· *It is good to find creative, appropriate ways to express our feelings, our hopes and dreams, and our ideas about ourselves.*

There is no healthier outlet for the expression of feelings than a compassionate listener. The security of knowing that there is someone we can talk to about whatever we're feeling, without fear of being judged, enables us to be more completely ourselves. For children to find such freedom in their families is an extraordinary gift. It may not be their parents who make the best confidants. That's why relationships with siblings, aunts and uncles, and grandparents are so important. We knit our families close so that somewhere in that circle of related souls a child may find a friend.

When our children are able to recognize and articulate their feelings, no matter what those feelings are, they are taking an important step in self-awareness, and the first step toward self-acceptance and acceptance of others.

Often, however, our children do not seem to be aware of their own feelings. This is not at all unusual; adults themselves are often blind to the emotions behind their actions. The psychiatrist Stanley Greenspan and the writer Amy Cunningham wrote in the *Washington Post:* "If you ask people who behave impulsively and aggressively how they're feeling, they probably won't express their feelings at all and may speak only of sequencing actions. For example, 'I hit him six times' becomes the answer to the question 'How did you feel?' . . . In good circumstances, the capacity to form a mental picture of wishes and feelings develops between 18 and 30 months and keeps developing in more complicated ways thereafter. But many young people never acquire the ability to picture their feelings and are thereby unable to fully contemplate their actions in advance. When challenged, such individuals respond with impulses and behavior—the hit, for instance—instead of simply feeling."

Adults and children alike often respond to questions about feelings with statements about thoughts. A man who had just heard a doctor give his mother a couple of months to live was asked what he felt, and he answered, "I wasn't surprised." A child watching cartoons says, "I don't like that monster," instead of "I'm scared of that monster."

When we add the word "like" to statements about how we feel, we are usually not talking at all about how we feel, but rather about what we think. "I feel like it's going to rain" has nothing to do with feelings. When our comments target "you" or "they," as in "I feel like you don't like me," they are closer to accusations than feelings.

Our children's feelings will find expression whether they want them to or not. Loneliness and insecurity can be disguised by attention-getting behaviors. Fear is often the cause of a child's stubborn resistance. Grief may be at the root of a child's self-isolation. But we are parents, not psychologists. It's not our business to probe the depths of our children's subconscious. We can, however, allow them the tools, time, and freedom to learn who they are and accept how they feel.

Many children who do not talk easily about their feelings can find creative expression for their emotions through writing, drawing, sculpting, sports, dance, acting, or music. And we can demonstrate that feelings can be safely expressed by appropriately expressing our own feelings. Most of all, we can give children time and freedom to become who they are, for we know from experience that it is the discoveries we make about ourselves, not what others tell us, that have the most meaning for our lives.

· *Feelings aren't forever. We can change the way we feel by taking a different perspective, practicing new habits, and having faith that change is possible.*

So much depends on how we choose to look at things. When we learn that it's possible to change our perspective on our lives, we become capable of changing the way we feel and act. This was a revelation to me, and it coincided with my amazing discovery that good days and bad days are not really determined by what happens in them. It was raining for the third day in a row and workmen were pulling up the carpet, moving all the furniture in my office, while I was trying to meet a pressing deadline. On some other day, the rain, the disruption, or the work—any one of them—would have been enough to put me in a foul, fretful mood. But this day, I happened to be feeling fine. None of it bothered me. There was absolutely nothing happening on the outside that made this day OK. The change was inside. And it was enough. The only drawback to my discovery is that I can no longer honestly blame other people and circumstances when I'm irritable.

The responsibility we exercise over our emotions can save our lives. Doctors know that cancer patients who meet their disease with hope and confidence instead of anger and self-pity live longer. Dr. Martin Luther King, Jr., survived two bombings of his house, a stabbing, five jailings, and daily death threats with his hope and generosity intact, only because he refused to sacrifice his inner peace for the revenge and hatred these injustices seemed to call for.

"As my sufferings mounted," King wrote, "I soon realized that there were two ways that I could respond to my situation: either to react with bitterness or seek to transform the suffering into a creative force. I decided to follow the latter course . . . If only to save myself from bitterness, I have attempted to see my personal ordeals as an opportunity to transform myself . . . I have lived these last few years with the conviction that unearned suffering is redemptive."

Frustration and Anger

Some feelings are more important to manage than others. Anger, guilt, shame, resentment, fear—these emotions can destroy us from the inside and do great harm to others if we don't identify them, express them, and set our sights past them.

Next to love, perhaps the most common emotion of children (and parents, as well) is frustration. Coincidentally, one of the strongest emotional indicators of prejudice in a personality is the inability to handle frustration. People with high levels of prejudice usually have low tolerance for frustration. When they cannot complete a task in time, when they are faced with problems that have no solutions, when they are given confusing or ambiguous instructions, their fear and insecurity surge and are expressed as frustration. They give up, get angry, or show other signs of stress. Frustration that persists easily transforms itself into anger, and anger always finds a target—in ourselves or in another human being. We've all experienced this.

Young Calvin was being typically candid with his pal Hobbes one day when he confessed, "I wish I had a baby brother."

"You want a new friend to play with?" Hobbes asked.

"No, I want somebody small I could beat up on."

Children have all kinds of opportunities to feel frustrated. Much that we expect of young children is very difficult for them. Toilet training, shoe-tying, subtraction, just being quiet—all are enormously challenging tasks in their daily lives. We can help our children find more comfortable ways of dealing with frustrations.

Five-year-old Jeffrey is sitting in the middle of the kitchen floor, trying to tie his shoes, while his father cooks. His fingers are chubby and clumsy, and he confuses the two strings in his hands. His father is giving him step-by-step instructions, very patiently, as he stirs the spaghetti, but Jeffrey is getting nowhere. Suddenly there's a scream and two high-top tennis shoes go flying across the room. Patient Dad picks them up and says calmly, "There's no reason to get upset. Calm down and try again. You'll get it."

What Dad says is nonsense, and Jeffrey knows it. Whether or not there's a reason for it (and for him, there's a *very* good reason), he is upset. And the last thing he feels like doing is "try again." Dad, in his great wisdom, knows that it takes practice and patience to learn to tie shoes. What he doesn't seem to understand is that you can't change feelings with words. What Jeffrey needed was some kind of acknowledgment that the job was incredibly difficult, that when we try to do difficult things we often get frustrated, and that when our frustration gets in the way of our accomplishing what we want to do, it's a good idea to try something different, like asking for help or going barefoot, or just taking a break and saving the lesson for later.

How often do we say "Don't worry" to someone who's afraid, or "Cheer up" to someone who's sad—as if the idea never occurred to him and all he needed were the proper instructions? We're not helpful not because we don't care, but because we lack imagination. As soon as we can remember being really frustrated or truly depressed ourselves, we know how ridiculous the words "Calm down" and "Cheer up" sound to others, including our children. Feelings need to be acknowledged before effective problem-solving can begin.

There are things we know from experience and can teach our children about uncomfortable feelings.

1. It's normal to be selfish. A Tears for Fears song title says it simply: "Everybody Wants to Rule the World." We want what we want when we want it, and we are disappointed when people do not act as we want them to. Much of our selfishness comes from insecurity. We are afraid that things will go wrong, that we won't get what we need. If our desires or fears are strong enough, we will try to control people and manipulate situations to get what we want.

2. When we are frustrated, jealous, depressed, or angry, it's generally because things did not happen the way we wanted them to. We didn't get what we wanted or someone didn't act as we wanted him to, or we're afraid things aren't going our way.

3. We often take out our frustrations and anger on another person or a group of people, even when we don't mean to. Of course, we usually end up feeling bad about ourselves—ashamed—when we do this, and our frustration or anger increases.

4. An easier way to live is to accept that things won't

always go the way we want them to, that we may be sad about it for a moment, but that everything will be all right. It is no one else's responsibility to make us happy, to satisfy our desires. Trying to manipulate others into giving us what we want will only make things worse. All we can do is express our feelings of frustration and then try to let them go.

These ideas are easy to communicate to our children once we become aware of the endless opportunities our own lives offer to use this knowledge. We can help them understand how feelings work by telling them about our own experiences: "I was so frustrated at work today. I couldn't get everything done that I needed to do, and I was mad at myself. I didn't even know I was mad until I yelled at you for slamming the door."

A Lesson in Tolerance

John Roberts had to bring some of the most difficult lessons of tolerance to his fourth-grade classroom one spring day in 1991. His students, mostly African Americans and Latinos, had "adopted" an African American sailor who was serving in the Persian Gulf: Petty Officer 3rd Class Harold Mansfield, Jr. They wrote letters to Mansfield, kept his photograph on the bulletin board, and drew pictures of his ship, the USS Saratoga. When the war ended and Mansfield returned safely home, the children greeted him with three hundred balloons and delivered laudatory speeches they had written.

Three weeks later, Mansfield was dead—shot and killed by a white supremacist named George David Loeb in a grocery store parking lot in Florida. Roberts, a former school counselor, didn't spend a long time planning what to say to his nine- and ten-year-olds. He gathered his children on the carpeted floor of his classroom. Then:

> I just told them a horrible thing that happened and we'd have to talk about it. I don't think you should ever shelter children from the truth. I gave the children the information I had. I put the words *white supremacist* on the board, and I had each child get a dictionary. We looked up *supremacist;* we talked about this, and we talked about our feelings.
>
> At first they wanted to strike back in the same way this man had attacked Harold. They wanted to kill him. They wanted to fry him in the electric chair. They wanted to drown him. All the horrible things you can imagine, they wanted to do those things. After we got through their anger, I said, "Boys and girls, let's be real. We don't work like that in our society. What would be some way we can positively let George David Loeb know that what he did was wrong and it hurt us?" Several of the children raised their hands and a discussion evolved, and they said, "We believe we should write to him."
>
> In their letters, the children's feelings ran the gamut, the same that adults do. Some were really wanting him to die, and at the other end of the spectrum were children who wanted to forgive him. A couple of them had nightmares.
>
> One girl wrote, "I don't think Mr. Roberts has forgiven you

and I don't think some of the children have forgiven you, but I forgive you. I just wish you hadn't killed Harold."

Children are so specific in their sense of justice and fairness. Some just wrote "We hope that you stay in jail forever."

By writing letters to the murderer of their hero, the children found a forceful and direct way to express their anger. A week later, school was out and they were on summer vacation. What they learned in fourth grade would always be with them: that some people hate others enough to kill them, for no reason except the color of their skin; that it is all right to say exactly how we feel about things; and that no matter how angry we get at the injustice of the world, we must find peaceful ways to express that anger.

Balance

What does tolerance feel like? What moves in our hearts in those moments when we greet the world without fear, distrust, anger, or resentment? Certainly it is more than a benign disinterest, a reprieve from pain. While we may not mistake it for a state of perfect contentment, tolerance is not boring.

Gordon Allport, in describing the tolerant person, listed "above all, a basic security and ego-strength" as the defining characteristic. "The core of the matter seems to be that every living being is trying to complete his own nature . . . His quest may take one of two roads. One road calls for safety

through exclusion . . . That person clings to a narrow island, restricts his circle, sharply selects what reassures him,
and rejects what threatens him. The other road is one of
relaxation, self-trust, and, therefore, trust of others. There is
no need to exclude strangers from one's gathering. Self-love
is compatible with love of others. This tolerant orientation is
possible because security has been experienced in the realistic handling of conflicts and social transactions. Unlike the
prejudiced person, the tolerant person does not perceive the
world as a jungle where men are basically evil and dangerous."

Self-trust is gained only through honest self-examina-
tion. The psychologist Erich Fromm described it in his classic work *Escape from Freedom:* "As a child, every human
being passes through a state of powerlessness, and truth is
one of the strongest weapons of those who have no power.
But the truth is in the individual's interest not only with
regard to his orientation in the outer world; his own strength
depends to a great extent on his knowing the truth about
himself. Illusions about oneself can become crutches useful
to those who are not able to walk alone; but they increase a
person's weakness. The individual's greatest strength is based
on the maximum of integration of his personality, and that
means also on the maximum of transparence to himself.
'Know thyself' is one of the fundamental commands that
aim at human strength and happiness."

Part of the comfort we feel in knowing ourselves comes
from our awareness that we are part of something much
greater than ourselves. The world does not revolve around

us, and whatever we're going through today will pass. With this awareness is born an inner source of strength that helps us transcend mere circumstances and come to feel the essence that is our life.

Psychologist Thomas Cottle observed children in desperate circumstances demonstrating moments of utter joy, and could only attribute it to their "mining something unique and wondrous about themselves from some inner shaft."

Something keeps us going, something that is available to us no matter what our talents, color, income, or circumstances. We are alike in what keeps us alive. When we touch that source of life strength, the differences between us are diminished. We experience something that tells us we are more beautiful than any notion we can have of ourselves, and capable of more than we imagine.

Parents who cannot transmit this understanding to their children, can, at least, offer hope that their children will find it themselves.

In *Nightlights: Bedtime Stories for Parents in the Dark,* Phyllis Theroux describes an exchange with her son. "At one particularly rough time during my older son's adolescence, I recorded a conversation we had in the kitchen when I simply said, 'I know that you feel in total darkness now, and that's confusing. But please believe me that it is only temporary. One day there will be light.'

"He sighed, nodded his head, and said, 'It couldn't be more confusing now.'

" 'I know,' I confirmed. 'That's what is so awful about

darkness.' End of conversation. Yet in all the conversations a parent has with one's children it seems increasingly important to me to give children our assurance that we have endured their same confusions and emerged to feel the sun on our backs."

Parenting is a constant process of letting go. We learn by letting go that our children will find joy in the most unexpected moments, and that they will go through desperate heartaches that we cannot prevent. And through the joys and heartaches that are theirs alone, they will find strength beyond our imagining to become who they are. We are, for a short time, the guardians of their lives, but we are not their makers. We can continue to be companions on their journeys only if we allow them to walk by themselves.

~

JOURNAL NOTES
CHAPTER 7

1. **Feelings are value-neutral.** What feelings do you try hardest never to express? Why? How do you view yourself when you have those feelings? Where do you think these judgments come from?

2. **Affirming feelings.** Think of a situation in which your child displays the feelings that bother you most. What would your usual reaction be—what would you think and

what would you say? Consider how you might respond differently to let your child know that it's OK to have such feelings.

3. Blaming others. Recall a day recently when you blamed someone else for the way you felt. What was the result of placing the responsibility for your emotional state on someone else?

4. Self-expression. Looking back at your answer to the first question, list three creative ways by which you might express the feelings you find most uncomfortable.

5. Wholeness. Describe a time when you felt inner joy. How did you view yourself and your relationship to others? How did you view the rest of the world? What thoughts, feelings, and actions do you associate with that experience?

To Live
What We Know

Unless we live what we know,
we do not even know it.
THOMAS MERTON

The kindergartners in Vivian Paley's class always discuss the important issues facing their classroom. So in 1990, when Mrs. Paley suggested a new rule—You Can't Say You Can't Play—meaning that no one had the right to exclude anyone else from play, several weeks of debate ensued. The kindergartners pitted the principle of democracy ("Let anybody play if someone asks") against the ideal of individual liberty ("But then what's the whole point of playing?"). They reflected on personal biases ("There's some people I don't like") and the consequences of victimization ("People that is alone they has water in their eyes.")

Most of them, as well as the older schoolchildren who were consulted, concluded that the new rule was just. But they were equally certain that it would never work. As one first-grader put it, "It's very fair. But people aren't that fair as the rule is."

As the debate went on, the children explored possible compromises to the rule of universal inclusion. They considered enacting the rule only if someone was crying, only if he or she "really really can't find someone else to play," only if it's not "too special" a game.

By talking about their new rule, the children were learning a great deal; they were growing in empathy and awareness of others, and they were beginning to develop new ways of thinking about rights and responsibilities. But they were not, as yet, actually following the rule.

As the time approached for the rule to go into effect in their classroom, a worried little girl asked, "At the end of the talking do we have to do it, or can we keep talking?"

"Yes," Mrs. Paley told Lisa, "after the talking, we *must* do it."

Without abandoning their thoroughly skeptical analysis of the new rule, the children began trying to practice it. And they learned by experience something that their very best thinking had denied: equal play *was* possible.

There are some things we can learn only by doing. When we talk about fairness, tolerance, and respect, we seem to know what we're talking about. We have in our minds a conception of what it means to be fair. But we can *know* what it means to be fair only when we have felt ourselves doing it. This is the lesson that Mrs. Paley wanted her children to learn.

The kindergartners discovered through practicing their new rule that their worst fears were unfounded: their play was not ruined; they were not forced to constantly change their games to accommodate a growing number of participants; they were still able to play with the people they liked; and they could even have fun with people they didn't like. They would never have learned these lessons by talking about fairness. They had to do it.

Like the kindergartners, we do not like to do what we don't feel like doing. But if we believe that fairness is right and that it is possible, then we must act fairly whether or not we feel like it. And by so doing, we sometimes find that our feelings imitate our actions. We can learn to feel kindly by acting kindly.

The anthropologist Mary Catherine Bateson experienced through her work the power of disciplined action to invite new ways of thinking and feeling. Life in Iran and Israel and the Philippines required her to learn to "feel and express culturally appropriate emotions," not by faking the feelings, but by practicing the behaviors that led to the feelings. "Some kinds of understanding grow only in repeated participation in forms that are not fully understood."

Aristotle would agree: "We become just by the practice of just actions, self-controlled by exercising self-control, and courageous by performing acts of courage . . . Hence it is no small matter whether one habit or another is inculcated in us from early childhood; on the contrary, it makes a considerable difference, or rather, all the difference."

Styles of Guidance

Despite the youngsters' fears, several things enabled Mrs. Paley's kindergartners to take the risk of trying something new. First, they were invited to express all their feelings and ideas about the new rule and what it would mean in their lives. They knew their ideas were listened to and considered. Second, they were shown examples, through made-up stories and their own experience, of the harm that is done when such a rule is not in place. Third, they were told in no uncertain terms that this was a rule and they must follow it.

It was not the rule itself, but the manner by which they were led to understand the rule, that enabled the children to obey it. In this story is an important lesson for parents: as eager as we are to see our children develop habits of acting and speaking in the spirit of caring, we must be careful how we attempt to guide them. For it is our manner of guiding them, more than the goal we're striving for, that will most significantly influence their values.

The research on prejudice offers indisputable evidence that intolerance in adults is closely linked to the way they were disciplined as children. The common denominator researchers have found among most prejudiced people is a family background of harsh and threatening parental discipline.

People who act out of intolerance, wrote the psychologist Elliott Aronson in *The Social Animal,* "tend to have parents who use love and its withdrawal as their major way of producing obedience. [They] . . . fear their parents and feel unconscious hostility against them. This combination sets the stage for the emergence of an adult with a high degree of anger, which, because of fear and insecurity, takes the form of displaced aggression against powerless groups, while the individual maintains an outward respect for authority."

Although the research on prejudice indicts harsh disciplinary techniques, we also know that permissiveness or negligence in response to inappropriate behavior is no more effective in promoting tolerance. Adults who feel acceptance and respect for others were raised in homes where discipline was firm, calm, and consistent; and where their relations with their parents were characterized by empathy, love, and mutual respect. They knew the moral rules their parents tried to live by, and they knew that breaking those rules involved consequences.

It's a frustrating and precarious position to be in, trying to make another person behave the way we desire. We find it quite easy to judge the behavior of other people, especially those closest to us, and we are tremendously tempted to correct them when we think they're wrong, either through argument, subtle manipulations, or punishment. For parents, that temptation is sometimes powerful to the point of compulsion. Our children, after all, lack the wisdom and experience that we bring to life and they need our guidance if they are to learn how to act civilly.

But just because our children need our direction doesn't mean that they are going to take it. We know how unimaginably difficult it can be to behave in ways we don't feel like behaving: to forgive a friend who has betrayed us, for instance, or to refrain from judging a person's character by his appearance. There are times, as well, when our children are unable to do what we ask of them. And there are times when they are able but not willing. We can have expectations for our children, but we cannot force them to meet our expectations. We can set rules for them, but we cannot keep them from breaking our rules. We can be comfortable in our roles as family leaders only when we accept that our children won't always follow where we lead.

Our attempts to guide our children's behavior will fail unless they take place in a context of tolerance. The moral principles we want our children to follow, we must also abide by. The respect and caring we expect from them, we must also give.

There are some general guidelines we can follow to help us practice tolerance even as we help our children practice it.

· *Involve children in family decisions and responsibilities.*
Mrs. Paley, like many teachers and a growing number of parents, depends on the children to take an active role in the responsibilities and decisions that affect the group. And

children, even those as young as four, have proven that they are fully up to the job. In the process, they learn to practice fairness, respect, communication, problem-solving, cooperation, and self-discipline.

When the adults in the family make all the decisions, lay down all the rules, impose all the rewards and punishments, children are robbed of the chance to practice moral responsibility and they come to feel like second-class citizens in the only society they know. They are little prepared to enter the larger society with any self-confidence or sense of responsibility.

It takes work to build a family, and children are just as much a part of that work as adults. Inviting children to participate in the work of family maintenance allows them to practice early the principles of equality and interdependence. They learn that others depend on their doing what they have agreed to do, that they are just as important as, but no more important than, everyone else in the family.

· *Offer children simple, firm rules by which they can judge their behavior.*

For young children, family rules offer an assurance that their lives are not limitless: someone else cares enough to protect them from harm and to help them learn how to live with others. For older children, the power of rules is largely in the temptation to challenge them. But all children follow rules more easily when they are involved in making them.

Rules, we should let our children know, are designed to help us remember our duties to one another. They are not designed for punishment. Adults, just as much as children, need rules to guide them. The longer we practice moral guidelines, the more natural they will become and the more uncomfortable we will feel in breaking them.

To guide our relationships with each other, inside and outside the family, the Golden Rule may be the only rule we ever need. It covers almost every aspect of human behavior and it has been applied in every culture. Versions of the Golden Rule are found in Christianity, Judaism, Islam, Buddhism, Confucianism, and Hinduism.

As simple as it seems, the idea of doing "unto others as you would have them do unto you" needs to be discussed and examined in families. Why, for instance, do we say "as you would have them do to you" instead of "as they do to you"? What's wrong with treating someone the way they treat you? If someone's cruel to me, why is it necessary for me to be kind to him?

One answer is that the Golden Rule helps us care for ourselves. We are happy and content when we follow it, and we are lonely and afraid when we don't follow it. By treating others as we want them to treat us, we are being people we can be proud of. We are demonstrating that we care about our principles and are unwilling to compromise them in the face of adversity.

Another area for discussion is how the Golden Rule works in our family. It means, for example, that if I want you to listen to me, I must listen to you. If I want you to help me, I must help you. If I want you to respect my needs, I must respect yours. If I treat you with attention, caring, respect, and love, it will be easier for you to treat me that way.

With the Golden Rule as a guide, we'll find answers to all kinds of dilemmas. What do we do when our friends put down another person or leave her out of a game? What do we do when we hear ethnic jokes? What do we do when someone uses a racial slur against another person? We simply put ourselves in the victim's place and imagine what would we want someone else to do, and then do that thing.

All other rules follow from the Golden Rule. For young children, one simple rule we can offer is "Don't hurt." We should make sure they are told explicitly the kinds of things that hurt: all kinds of violence (hitting, spitting, biting, scratching, slapping, kicking, and so on) and many kinds of words (name-calling, taunting, threats, and lies).

· *Provide natural and logical consequences when rules are broken.*

The only really effective discipline is self-discipline. When children have a sense of what's right and wrong, when they are confident about who they are and who they want to be, they are able to refrain from most serious offenses. They feel responsible for their own actions and confident that they can make their own decisions about their behavior. Parents who clearly communicate the values of tolerance, and who give their children choices rather than exercise dictatorial control over their actions, are helping their children develop a sense of responsibility and a habit of self-discipline.

When rules are broken or mistakes made, it's critically important that parents use consequences, rather than punishment, as a means for changing behavior.

Children who are punished harshly or inconsistently, or who are frequently threatened with punishment, are prevented from developing the internal controls they need to discipline themselves. Punishment demeans its target and diminishes the self-esteem necessary for true moral strength. It is an act of retribution that demonstrates power, authority, and superiority over the victim. We punish others because we want to make them hurt more than we want to help them change. People who are punished for their wrongdoings typically feel ashamed, resentful, and angry. Rather than focusing on the changes they need to make, they focus on the harm that was done to them. Their only motive for changing their behavior becomes the fear of punishment, rather than an internal mandate of conscience.

Consequences, on the other hand, are the natural outcomes of our misbehavior. If we are late to work every day because we don't feel like getting out of bed in the morning, we'll lose our jobs. If we don't pay our bills, we'll lose our possessions. If we act unkindly to those around us, we'll lose our friends. Most of the everyday transgressions of children have painful consequences that can be powerful incentives for change as long as we don't interfere with those consequences. It's not necessary for us to lecture, yell at, or punish a child who refuses to eat breakfast. All we have to do is refrain from serving him special meals. His hunger will teach him to eat when meals are served.

Our primary motive for all discipline should be to promote self-discipline—something we learn naturally when we experience the consequences of our actions. When we regulate our own actions because we want to, not in order to please someone else, we achieve a true moral competence.

My four-year-old friend was beginning to learn that she was responsible for her own actions the day she announced to her mom, "I don't want to talk to Santa Claus this year."

"OK," her mother said, "but why not?"

"Because I've been mean to you and Grandma and I don't want him to know about it."

Although she still felt answerable to Santa Claus for her behavior, she had internalized a moral rule and was independently choosing to accept the consequences of her misbehavior. Not talking to Santa Claus, in her mind, meant the likelihood of not getting what she wanted for Christmas.

· *Distinguish between what we can change and what we cannot change.*

Deciding how to respond to our children's behavior is one of the toughest challenges of parenting. It helps if we ask ourselves what we are trying to change and whether it is our responsibility to effect that change.

Some things, no matter how much we dislike them, are simply not in our power to alter. We can't change our children's personalities, their feelings, their thoughts or moods, nor their friendships, interests, talents. What we can change is our feeling that these things are under our control. Once we realize that our power over our children's lives is limited, we are freed from any obligation to engineer their futures, and we can focus on enjoying them as they are today.

Susan Corbett writes about refusing to buy her five-year-old daughter a Barbie doll. "It was my daughter's bad luck" that her request for a Barbie "coincided with my newly discovered awareness of my second-class status as a woman," wrote Corbett, in the May 1994 issue of *Young Children.* "I sanctimoniously announced that her parents would never shell out even a penny for Barbie." Nevertheless, her daughter received several of the coveted dolls for her birthday. Years later, Corbett discovered a large cache of Barbie clothes in her daughter's bedroom. "When I asked how an unemployed twelve-year-old had acquired them, she calmly replied that she had stolen them bit by bit from her friends. In my zealous self-centeredness to teach my little girl what I believed to be 'for her own good' as a female human being, I had inadvertently led her to an early career as a thief.

"*My* history, *my* biases, and *my* needs had become the modus operandi rather than the wishes of a child who merely wanted to play dolls with her friends."

If we respect the individuality of our children and accept that we are not their rulers but their guides, we can let go of our need to control the harmless details of their lives. We have no business dictating their friendships, clothing tastes, hair styles, music preferences, hobbies, or interests. We can offer them alternatives, express our own preferences, talk about why we feel the way we do, but ultimately we have to respect the choices they make—not because we agree with them, but because we support their efforts to discover and become, independently from us, who they are.

· *Examine our motives.*

Often we feel the urge to steer our children in the direction we would like them to go for reasons that have nothing to do with their happiness or well-being. We use the power of our own regrets, as Susan Corbett did, to try to redirect their interests.

Left to their own resources, children are often able to work out their differences, find solutions to frustrating problems, and comfort themselves without our intervention. Each time they do, they are experiencing important emotional growth that will serve them well in their relationships to themselves and others.

Our temptations to take things under control can be strong. Before we intervene, we should ask ourselves, "What are my motives?" If the situation threatens serious emotional or physical harm, there is no room for debate. We are motivated by instinct and reason to do what's necessary to make our children safe, or by our obligation to encourage self-discipline, self-awareness, and social responsibility.

But in most cases, the question is more complicated. "Parents and teachers don't like to admit that, often, the main reason they like to use punishment is to demonstrate their power to win over the child or to gain revenge by making the child suffer," wrote Jane Nelson in *Positive Discipline.*

When we use bribery, threats, punishment, deceit, manipulation, shame, or even violence, our goal is not to help our children learn how to change their behavior as much as it is to make our own lives easier or to satisfy an urge for revenge.

"Where did we ever get the crazy idea," wrote Nelson, "that in order to make children perform better, we must first make them feel worse?"

A fifteen-year-old daughter is stopped by the police and charged with speeding and driving without a license. Her father is embarrassed, angry, distrustful, and hurt. Several options occur to him: he can ground her, take away her telephone privileges, make her clean house on Saturday instead of going to the mall. His motives? He wants to instill fear and respect in her, show her who's boss, take revenge for his pain, exercise his authority. He decides to ground her, forcing her to miss basketball practice. She is cut from the team.

Yet he didn't really need to devise a punishment for his daughter's actions. He could have let her take responsibility for her own violation by paying the traffic fine and court costs, and contributing to the higher auto insurance costs that resulted from her violations.

· *Separate the person from the behavior.*

In any discussion about a problem between people, but especially with children, it's important to confine our judgment to the behavior that bothers us, and not judge the person. In all cases, we should make it clear that it's the child's action, not her character, that is a problem. And we must make this explicit: "I love you very much, but what you did really bothers me."

We can still be honest, firm, and respectful in stating our objections, the reasons for our objections, and the consequences that will result from the child's action. We don't have to compromise family rules or our own values. We don't have to hide our anger or disappointment. And we can make sure that serious infractions bring serious consequences. But through it all, we should remind our children that our love for them is not conditional on their behavior.

· *Begin by talking.*

Most of our responses to children's misbehavior begins with the word "don't." We see or hear something that irritates us, and something tells us that if we simply say "don't," they won't. Sometimes, but rarely, it's that simple.

More often, the behavior pauses for a moment or a day, and then begins again. For a child to respond well to "don't," that "don't" must be fully discussed and understood. The reasons behind the rules must be made plain.

We have plenty of opportunities to open discussions with our children about the reasons for tolerant behavior. Young children, especially, express their biases quite openly, through name-calling, violence, exclusion, and other acts of meanness. We won't usually be around when such incidents occur, but when we are, we should always take action.

The guidelines here can be adapted to respond to various acts of bias as well as other conflicts between younger children.

1. *Interrupt the action.* Step into it calmly and quietly, take the children's hands, or offer them a gentle touch. Let them know in a calm but firm voice that it's time to talk. Lead them to a quiet place where you can all sit down together. Ask them to sit quietly for just a minute, and take a moment to remind yourself to remain friendly, calm, and firm.

2. *Remind children about the rules.* No hurting, no name-calling, no pushing, no hitting. Disagreements are allowed, but meanness is not.

3. *Recall the reasons for the rules.* Calling someone a name or talking bad about them hurts their feelings. We don't like to have our own feelings hurt, and it's not good for us to hurt someone else's feelings either.

4. *Identify and share feelings.* Listen carefully to all the children, one at a time, and help them name the feelings they have. Try to bypass the accusations and denials, and help them focus on what they feel.

5. *Affirm their feelings.* "It's OK for you to feel ——" (name the feeling). Try to identify with their feelings by sharing a similar experience you have had.

6. *Remind them that they have choices.* "We can all decide what to do with our feelings. Usually it helps to share them with someone we can talk to. But we

know that we don't have the right to express them by hurting someone else. What else can we do when we feel this way?" Repeat their suggestions and offer some of your own. Ask the other child or children involved: "What do you do when you feel ——?"

7. *Heal the victim.* In the case of name-calling, for instance, first give the victim a chance to explain what was said and how it felt. Second, tell the victim in no uncertain terms that "what she said was a very ugly name. It's not OK to say things like that here, no matter how angry we are. You are not a ——. You are a beautiful person and I love you. When you hear someone say that name, you need to remind yourself that they are wrong, that they have a problem—maybe they're mad or their feelings are hurt—and you can always tell them 'You don't have a right to call me that.' "

You may also need to explain, "Some grown-ups use those words because they're not happy about themselves and they need to look down on someone else. Sometimes children hear them from grownups and they use those words when they're angry. Sometimes they don't even mean them. But whatever reason they use them, the words are ugly." Offer them a slogan to remember whenever someone says something to hurt their feelings: "Tell yourself, 'Just because someone says it doesn't mean it's true.' "

8. *Make a plan.* For each of them, agree together that

the next time they feel that way, they will make a decision to take some specific action. They can remind each other of the rules; they can walk away from the scene; they can find another person to talk to about what happened; they can stop what they are doing; they can apologize; they can forgive. Tell them you will help remind them of their plans (and do it!).

9. *Offer a choice.* Ask them if they still want to play together. If one says no, honor that choice. If they do, tell them, "It's important after we hurt each other that we apologize for what we've done wrong and that we forgive the other person for what they've done wrong. The way it works is simple. One person says, 'I'm sorry I hurt your feelings,' and the other person says, 'I forgive you.' I'm going to leave you two to take care of that yourselves."

People are shaped by the virtues they rehearse, Mary Catherine Bateson learned as she entered other cultures. And Vivian Paley's children found it to be so. By practicing the acts of friendliness, they came to experience the feelings of friendship.

A fifth-grader described the practice of fairness: "It would take a lot of getting used to, but it could happen. Right now there's a lot of saying no, but if you kept at it a long time you could get it into your brain to say yes."

To get in the habit of being fair, adults as well as children need vigilance and patience and lots of practice. It means breaking old habits of thought and feelings as well as changing the way we behave. It means doing things differently from the way we've always done them. For children who have not yet learned that it's even possible to change habits or to act in ways that don't come naturally, practicing fairness is doubly hard. But Mrs. Paley's children, year after year, prove that it is possible. If five-year-olds can learn to treat one another kindly, surely there is hope for the rest of us.

⤙

Journal Notes
Chapter 8

1. Remembering rules. What were the clear *do's* and *don'ts* you grew up with? How did you come to learn them? Why did you obey them?

2. Punishment. Describe what you remember as the harshest punishment you ever received. What precipitated it? How did you feel about yourself? How did you feel about the punisher? How did the experience affect your subsequent actions?

3. In control? Describe a problem you have with your child. What is it that you object to? What would you like to change? Do you have the power to make that change? What realistic options do you have?

4. Reacting. When your child does something that surprises you in its immaturity or thoughtlessness, what are the first words that come to your mouth? What is your gut feeling? Do you think your reaction is effective? What might be a better way to respond?

5. Responding to bias. What biases do you see expressed by your children? How are they expressed? How can you responsibly respond to them?

A New Us

*We are caught in an inescapable
network of mutuality; tied in a single
garment of destiny . . . I can never be
what I ought to be until you are what
you ought to be. You can never be what
you ought to be until I am what I ought
to be. This is the way the world is
made. I didn't make it that way, but
this is the interrelated structure of
reality.*
DR. MARTIN LUTHER KING, JR.

In the aftermath of the Los Angeles riots, blacks and whites
and Asians passing on the streets didn't know what to say to
each other, so they walked by unspeaking, their eyes averted.
People who had formerly been friendly retreated into awk-

ward silence. When the jury pronounced O. J. Simpson not guilty of murder, blacks and whites had opposite reactions, and they quickly retreated into separate circles to share those thoughts.

At a Midwestern high school, students formed a club to address their racial divisions. To encourage more interaction between whites and blacks, they moved their single soda machine to the center of the "black" area of the student commons, where African American students habitually gathered. Then they watched in dismay as white students walked quickly to the soda machine, got their drinks, and walked back out, ignoring and ignored by black students.

This is how we've learned to deal with our differences. We walk into each other's lives to do our business, attend our classes, run our errands, but we don't stay long enough to get to know each other.

Today, the subjects of racism and prejudice are off-limits in mixed company. We seem to have chosen silence as the favored strategy for keeping peace—a silence that serves our fears but ultimately does not protect us. And it's just this silence that will bury us. We must break the silence. We must set ourselves and each other free to say what we think about the differences between us. We must create safe ways to tell our truths to each other.

Certainly, if we are to become our best selves, we must begin to make connections with others. As many people from all cultures and in all times have understood, we become fully human only in the context of community. We need each other in order to know who we are.

We see this most clearly in families, where, despite the essential mystery we present to each other, we become part of these other people. Even our closest relationships are marked by occasional misunderstandings, resentments, fears, and distrust. We are shocked when the person we thought we knew completely does something that violates our assumptions about them. But we find ways to maintain those relationships despite our disappointments. We forgive, we make allowances, we change, because we understand the importance of these people to our life. Even knowing that disappointments will come again, we sacrifice the safe emotional distance for the persistently uncertain company of those around us. Only the most deeply wounded of us can deny our own humanity enough to tell ourselves that we need no one.

Scientists, in their observation of the natural world, have developed a theory that may help explain, or at least serve as an appropriate metaphor for, human relationships. It's called chaos theory, and it holds, in part, that the workings of this planet are the result of an accumulation of tiny, seemingly unrelated events that can never be catalogued or quantified but that nevertheless have enormous consequences for all life. The smallest interactions between the species of life and the elements of nature work together in the most mysterious ways. Because we cannot determine just how those interactions work, the events of our world often appear to be unruly, chaotic, even cataclysmic.

If chaos theory remains controversial in science, it makes rather good sense in families and society. Each of us is a character made from a random collection of genes, shaped by culture, religion, economics, education, and all the important and incidental people and events in our lives. Affection given and lost, suffering escaped or endured, words spoken and left unspoken—each day we carry the profound influences of other people in ways we'll never fully understand.

In physics and in human relations, what looks like chaos on the outside disguises an intricate interdependence that's neither predictable or controllable. Whether we live together in peace or at odds, we cannot but live intertwined in ways we'll seldom know.

For the first-century Chinese philosopher Tu-Shun, the metaphor of the jeweled net of Indra described what physicists now refer to as the iterations of chaos. As translator Stephen Mitchell explains: "The Net of Indra is a profound and subtle metaphor for the structure of reality. Imagine a vast net; at each crossing point there is a jewel; each jewel is perfectly clear and reflects all the other jewels in the net, the way two mirrors placed opposite each other will reflect an image ad infinitum. The jewel in this metaphor stands for an individual being, or an individual consciousness, or a cell, or an atom. Each jewel is intimately connected with all other jewels in the universe, and a change in one jewel means a change, however slight, in every other jewel."

For the twentieth-century writer Wendell Berry, the understanding that our diverse lives are intertwined came as the result of a personal quest to understand the damage of racism. Berry wrote ". . . no man is alone, because *he can-*

not be; he cannot arrange it so that either the good or the bad effects of his life will apply only to himself; he can only live in the creation, among the creatures, his life either adding to the commonwealth or subtracting from it."

And Martin Luther King, Jr., spoke often about the reality of our relationships to each other. "The universe is so structured that things do not quite work out rightly if men are not diligent in their concern for others," he said. "The self cannot be self without other selves. I cannot reach fulfillment without thou. Social psychologists tell us that we cannot truly be persons unless we interact with other persons. All life is interrelated."

What poets have known is that our great diversity can make a stronger bond, not a weaker one, and a world of unfathomable beauty.

"Glory be to God for dappled things," wrote the poet Gerard Manley Hopkins, who saw in our mottled creation a wondrous complexity. Dappled things we are, individually and collectively, and quite remarkable for that dappling. In our diversity is mystery and wonder, and, at times, confusion, conflict, and distrust.

We should take neither too much joy nor too much discouragement in the recent revelations of our differences. They are less important to our own health and the health of this world than the things we share.

For it is what we share that will save us, individually and collectively. If we cannot identify our common ideals, and sense our common need for each other, we cannot feel a part of the community, we cannot feel responsible for its preservation. The work we do in our hearts will produce benefits that reach beyond our own lives into the lives of others. We cannot know what those benefits will be, but we can be assured that by changing ourselves, we are doing the only thing we can do to change the world. To say that it is not enough is a lack of will, a lack of faith. It must be enough, for it is everything.

Just as Gordon Allport offered us an understanding of the harm intolerance does to ourselves, Martin Luther King Jr. offered us a vision of community and a rationale for reconciliation that can guide us toward unity. It has been nearly half a century since he spoke, but his words still ring true.

> We have learned through the grim realities of life and history that hate and violence solve nothing. They only serve to push us deeper and deeper into the mire. Violence begets violence; hate begets hate; and toughness begets a greater toughness. It is all a descending spiral, and the end is destruction—for everybody. Along the way of life, someone must have enough sense and morality to cut off the chain of hate by projecting the ethics of love into the center of our lives . . .
>
> I've seen too much hate on the faces of too many Klansmen . . . to want to hate myself, because every time I see it, I know that it does something to their faces and their personalities and I say to myself that hate is too great a burden to bear. I have decided to love.

Perhaps parents, more than anyone, know what it means to say, "I have decided to love." Can we make the same sort of decision for the sake of our communities that we make daily for our family's sake?

⤸

JOURNAL NOTES
CHAPTER 9

1. **Unity.** Describe one group you are a part of. What thoughts and feelings do you have about the members that help unite you with them? What thoughts and feelings do you have that would separate you? What is the most important thing that you share?

2. **Visualize community.** Draw a symbolic design of community that helps you visualize your interdependence on one another.

3. **Write a poem** that evokes your feelings of being at home with others.

4. **Shared treasures.** Make a list of the five things that are most important to you. Which of these do you think are shared by people the world over? What is the meaning of this observation in terms of your feelings toward people of other cultures?

5. **Unique or universal?** Henry David Thoreau wrote, "It is my growing conviction that my life belongs to others as much as it belongs to myself and that what is experienced as most unique often proves to be most solidly embedded in the common condition of being human." Recall the experiences you've had that you felt unable to communicate accurately in words, the times you've wanted to tell someone, "But you don't understand!" What were the experiences and the emotions surrounding them? What aspects of those experiences can you identify as universal?

FAMILY ACTIVITIES

We help strengthen the feelings associated with tolerance—confidence, compassion, trust, empathy, humility, serenity—by consciously practicing acts of caring as a family. This is a shared adventure in learning, a gentle journey in which you make experience the teacher.

Here are some suggested exercises.

Belonging

· Blend the principles of tolerance into your religious, cultural, or family rituals and traditions through scriptures, music, and artifacts of different cultures. Take time to honor your ideals in ways that are explicit, predictable, and routine, as well as on special occasions. Incorporate elements of other cultural celebrations into your own cultural holidays.

· Look through family photo albums together and teach your child about their relatives, past and present. Relate memories and stories about the people in the photos, point out special traits that are shared across generations, and identify characteristics that your child has in common with other relatives.

· Share memories of your own past, and stories that have been passed down from your relatives.

· Circulate a blank book among your relatives, asking them to write down special memories from your family past and to say something to your children about their value to the family.

· Post photos in your child's room of grandparents, parents, siblings, and friends.

· Write notes and cards to your children occasionally, reminding them of your love and appreciation for them.

· Share letters from distant family members with your children. Pass on to your children news from relatives and friends.

· Do a family-tree poster that your child can color and hang in her room.

· Read stories relating to your ethnic, cultural, and religious heritage.

· Take your children to museum exhibitions, cultural festivals, and musical performances that display aspects of your heritage.

· Help strengthen your child's connection to others by supporting their involvement in sports, school, neighborhood, and church activities.

· Hug them often, and tell them you love them.

The Language of Caring

· Use words of tolerance with your children daily. In addition to teaching them the forms of civility—"Please" and "Thank you"—teach them the language of appreciation, caring, respect, and forgiveness—"I'm sorry," "You're right," "I forgive you," "I like you," "Can I help?" "Let's cooperate," "Let's compromise."

· Discuss how words can hurt us. Use a storybook to introduce the idea if possible. Then tell your children about a time when you were teased, gossiped about, rejected, or called a name, and how the words that were used against you or someone else caused you pain. Brainstorm the names that people use to hurt each other (including put-downs and racial slurs). Agree that these words will not be used in your family.

Self-awareness

· With your children, create self-portraits using drawings, symbols, or words that depict not how you look, but how you feel.

· With poster board, a stack of old magazines, and an array of objects (buttons, feathers, yarn, paper clips, twigs, leaves), put together a collage entitled "The Me Inside Me."

· Take turns selecting music that expresses how you feel. Sing or dance if you feel like it.

· Play a game: "If I was an animal, I would be a ——

because . . ." "If I were a color . . ." "If I were a TV character . . ."

· Make up a story with your child as the main character, and ask your child to help you finish it.

· Inventory the day. At bedtime or suppertime, trade notes on the day with family members. What was your favorite thing about the day? What was your least favorite thing? What did you do that was kind? What did you do that was thoughtless?

· Offer older children an opportunity for private journal-writing by buying them their own blank books and sharing with them examples of how journal-writing has helped you understand yourself better. Assure them that if they choose to keep a journal, you will respect their privacy absolutely.

Expressing Feelings

· Help children identify feelings by looking at the faces in picture books and asking, "What do you think he or she feels like?"

· Family meetings can become opportunities for the safe expression of feelings if each member listens attentively and shares honestly. Let children know that whatever they are feeling is OK to talk about; that they won't be judged by their feelings. Emphasize the importance of claiming our own feelings rather than accusing others of "making" us feel certain ways. Then go around the room sharing simple feeling statements: "Today I felt —— when . . ."

Differences

· Play "Who am I?" Describe a friend or family member without saying the name, focusing mainly on personality traits, and have the children guess who it is.

· Help children compare skin tones, hair texture, size, and facial features to see how they look different. Point out the beauty in physical differences.

· Help children overcome the negative associations with dark colors by affirming the rich beauty of browns in nature, and by selecting dark colors when painting or coloring with them.

· Read about the diversity in nature to see how life comes in different forms, and to learn how all life depends on each other.

Thinking About Values

· Watch TV with your children; make comments and ask questions about what they think.

· Talk about the stories you read together.

· Draw connections between the events you see in daily life and on TV, and the rules and values that guide your family. Point out the harm caused by rules being broken.

· Repeat and discuss the following proverbs (and any others you've learned from your family). Talk about what they mean, explain that we use them to remind ourselves of how to act toward others. Offer examples and ask for examples of situations where we might need to tell ourselves these things.

> Don't judge another until you've walked a mile in their shoes.
>
> If you can't say anything nice, don't say anything at all.
>
> People in glass houses shouldn't throw stones.
>
> He ain't heavy; he's my brother.
>
> You can't judge a book by its cover.
>
> Do unto others as you would have them do unto you.
>
> It's not whether you win or lose, it's how you play the game.
>
> To have a friend, be a friend.
>
> What goes around comes around.
>
> As you sow, so shall you reap.
>
> We're all in the same boat.
>
> There, but for the grace of God, go I.

Changing Perceptions

· To help children see beyond society's stereotype of beauty, point out the attractiveness you see in people who are fat, old, disabled, bald, plainly dressed, un-madeup, and in people of all skin colors and facial features.

· Make a commitment to help each other check the ways they talk about other people or groups. Understand that everyone has a right to "check" everyone else, and that such checks will be considered a source of mutual help and guidance, not condemnation. Examples of comments that earn a "check that":

Categorical judgments. When we criticize someone by saying "You (or anyone) *always* or *never* . . ." we are pronouncing a prejudice. When we describe a group in global terms instead of what we know about individual members— "They're all . . ."—we are risking stereotypes.

Finding Perspective

· Use pretend play and storytelling to invite children to take on other personalities, find ways to explain what they don't understand, and test new ways of being and thinking. We promote their growth and independence by giving them absolute freedom of imagination at play, allowing them to be whoever they want to be.

· Storytelling also offers children an opportunity to exercise their imaginations by looking at the world from new perspectives. More than ever, children's books today reflect a variety of different cultures, encouraging youngsters to find common ground across differences. But we can also encourage new perspectives on favorite traditional stories by talking about the different characters: "I wonder what that Giant thought about Jack walking into his house?" "Do you think those stepsisters really liked being mean?" Or we can look for stories that send direct messages about different ways of seeing things, such as the Indian legend about the blind men and the elephant.

· For older children, as for ourselves, taking a different perspective means redefining some of the concepts that society hands down to us, such as our notions of beauty and success. We are so accustomed to success being defined by competition that we find it hard to see the success of those who meet their own challenges but don't come out in first place. When we insist on the glory of the effort as well as the victory, we offer our children different perspectives on entrenched stereotypes.

· Play "I wonder what it'd be like to [live in Brazil, be a ballet dancer, work on a farm, travel to the moon]." What would we eat? What would we wear? What would we do in our spare time? What would our friends be like? What would be different about us?

Critical Thinking

· Choose opposing sides of an issue that you are interested in. Set rules for fair arguing (don't interrupt, don't call names or raise voices, give everyone a chance to talk, and don't take it personally), and practice debating.

· Trade opinions with your teenager about events in the news, evaluating the available evidence on all sides.

· Generate discussions about the stereotypical messages you see on television or billboards. Advertising is a particularly rich source of irrational thinking.

Encourage Empathy

· Use role-reversals to help children understand another person's feelings and actions. If, for instance, your child excludes someone from play, have her imagine what it would feel like to be the excluded child. If two children are arguing about something, have them sit face to face, pretend each is the other person, and talk to each other about their feelings, thoughts, and actions. Or give each child paper and pencil and ask her to write about a situation from the other person's perspective, describing her experiences and feelings.

· Observe and talk about acts of caring, sharing, and respect that you see in others.

· Explain the values and feelings behind your own acts of compassion.

· Try an exercise called "Who Needs My Help?" (described in *Bringing Up a Moral Child*, by Schulman and Meeker). Ask your children to think of someone who needs their help, and to answer the questions, "When do they need help? Why do they need help? What help do they need? How can I help? When did I help?"

· Another exercise—"What Did I Do?"—can raise children's awareness of their own effect on other people. Have them answer the questions "What did I do today that made someone feel good?" and "What did I do today that made someone feel bad?" and talk about the feelings and reasons behind their actions.

Intolerance Observed

· It's important to take notice of the intolerance we see in ourselves and others. Brainstorm a list of intolerant behaviors (gossiping, name-calling, violence, rejection) and then for a week keep individual logs noting each time you see or hear about an example of these behaviors—whether it be in school, at home, in the neighborhood, or even on television. At your next meeting, go around the circle recalling the incidents one by one. Discuss how common, and how easy, intolerance is.

Family Responsibility

· Use family meetings to assign responsibilities for household duties for parents and children. Indicate your trust and respect for children by including responsibilities they enjoy. In addition to picking up their rooms and feeding the pets, for instance, children can be responsible for choosing rental movies and ordering pizza on Saturday nights.

· Use this exercise to simulate your family's dependence on and responsibility for one another. In a large open space, each family member brings ten sheets of paper on which he or she has written or drawn a problem or fear. Each person in turn wads each piece of paper into a ball and throws it out into the center of the group. They can all choose whether or not to share what they've put on paper before tossing it out. Then one person volunteers to be blindfolded and stands alone at one end of the space strewn with paper. The other family members are responsible for giving that person careful directions so that he or she can walk to the other side without stepping on a "problem." The guides are not allowed to touch the traveler. Their instructions must be precise, and the traveler is allowed to ask questions to clarify the directions. If the traveler succeeds in making it to the other side, everyone wins a hug. If the traveler falters, everyone involved in the game loses. After one person has traveled through, pass the blindfold on to the next person until everyone in the family has experienced the uncertainty, confusion, and reliance on others that comes with walking blind, and everyone has had the opportunity to feel responsible for helping each other through the obstacle course.

Social Responsibility

· Make a list of volunteer opportunities in your community, and let the children choose an activity for the family to participate in. You can tutor a recent immigrant in English, deliver meals to the homebound, read books to hospitalized children, collect blankets for a homeless shelter.

· Make a habit of regular charitable donations to an organization that you and the children choose together, after reading about and researching various alternatives.

· Hold a yard sale and let children decide how to spend the money in a way that will benefit others.

· Even though we may be deeply offended by the biases

that are expressed around us, we find it very difficult to openly oppose those biases. Talk about different ways to express your opposition to stereotyping—from refusing to join in put-downs to expressing opinions contrary to common assumptions. Role-play possible responses to racist jokes, sexual harassment, and other familiar types of prejudice.

Learning About Cultures

- Bring into your home dolls, games, books, movies, music, and artwork from different cultures (see Family Resources).
- Eat at a variety of ethnic restaurants, and let children help cook foods from different countries.
- Attend worship services of different faiths.
- Participate in the holiday celebrations and religious observances of different cultures. Learn about and enjoy Cinqo de Mayo, Kwanzaa, a Passover seder, a Chinese New Year, a Mormon Christmas Eve.
- Hold occasional family Teach-ins, where parents and children report on aspects of another culture's history, art, music, religion, or current events.
- Visit museums, historic districts, and archaeological sites to learn more about our country's multicultural heritage.
- Check the TV schedule for documentaries that can teach us about other cultures and lands, that reveal our own

nation's multicultural past, or that can help us reflect on the harm of prejudice and intolerance.

Making Connections

· Seek out integrated environments for yourself and your children—day care centers, schools, neighborhoods, churches, summer camps, volunteer organizations, sports leagues, community groups.

· Build friendships across traditional social boundaries. Avoid restricting your interactions at work, school, church, and community functions to people of your own age, race, income level, or regional background.

· Start an intercultural discussion group (see Organizations and Resources).

· Become pen pals with people in other parts of the country or the world, either through E-mail or the postal service.

ORGANIZATIONS
PROMOTING TOLERANCE

American Friends Service Committee
1501 Cherry Street
Philadelphia, PA 19102
(215) 241-7000
Advocates for social justice and racial harmony.

Anti-Defamation League of B'nai B'rith
823 UN Plaza
New York, NY 10017
(212) 490-2525
Educational resources on tolerance include A World of Difference program for schools.

Association of MultiEthnic Americans
1060 Tennessee Street
San Francisco, CA 94107
(415) 548-9300
National organization offers a list of local member organizations.

Children's Defense Fund
25 E Street NW
Washington, DC 20001
(800) 233-1200
The nation's most powerful lobbying group on behalf of
children, led by civil rights activist Marian Wright
Edelman, publishes a monthly newsletter and reports on
the status of children.

Corporation for National and Community Service
1100 Vermont Avenue NW
Washington, DC 20525
(202) 488-7378
Clearinghouse for information on community service
initiatives nationwide.

Family Resource Coalition
200 S. Michigan Avenue, 16th Floor
Chicago, IL 60604
(312) 341-0900
Resources for support groups and training in community-
building.

The Foundation for Community Encouragement
109 Danbury Road, Suite 8
Ridgefield, CT 06877
(203) 431-9484
FAX: (203) 531-9349
Conducts community-building workshops for
organizations. Founded by M. Scott Peck, M.D.

Generation to Generation
A Network for Families' Spiritual Nurture
PO Box 146
Millwood, NY 10546
Provides workshops and resources; headed by Jean Grasso
Fitzpatrick.

Center for Healing Racism
PO Box 27327
Houston, TX 77227
(713) 738-7223
Publications and workshops for community groups.

Interracial Family Circle
PO Box 53290
Washington, DC 20009
(800) 500-9040
Provides newsletter, resource list, and listing of interracial
support groups.

National Black Child Development Institute
1023 15th Street NW, Suite 600
Washington, DC 20005
(800) 556-2234
Provides research, lobbying, tutoring, and mentoring
programs for black children. Offers newsletter and other
publications.

The National Conference
71 Fifth Avenue, Suite 1100
New York, NY 10003
(212) 206-0006
Sponsors Anytown, an interracial retreat for teenagers.

The National Endowment for the Humanities
The National Conversation
Washington, DC 20277-2885
(202) 606-8400
Provides conversation kits for group discussions on
American pluralism and identity.

P-FLAG
(Parents, Families, and Friends of
Lesbians and Gays, Inc.)
1101 14th Street NW, Suite 1030
Washington, DC 20005
(202) 638-4200

Parent Action
Box 1719
Washington, DC 20013-1719
(410) 752-7140
Opportunities for community service and national
lobbying on behalf of parents and children.

Parenting for Peace and Justice Network
Institute for Peace and Justice
4144 Lindell Boulevard, Room 124
St. Louis, MO 63108
(314) 533-4445
Provides a newsletter, workshops, family camps, and
resources for local family support groups.

Simon Wiesenthal Center
9760 West Pico Boulevard
Los Angeles, CA 90035
(310) 553-9036
Sponsors the Museum of Tolerance and offers Holocaust
resources.

Study Circles Resource Center
PO Box 203, 697 Pomfret Street
Pomfret, CT 06258
(860) 928-2616
Offers detailed workshop manuals for facilitating group
discussions on race relations and violence.

Sunrise Books, Tapes & Videos
PO Box B
Provo, UT 84603
(800) 456-7770
Offers information workshops, lectures, and study group
aids by Jane Nelson, author of *Positive Discipline.*

Teaching Tolerance
The Southern Poverty Law Center
400 Washington Avenue
Montgomery, AL 36104
(334) 264-0286
Publishes twice-yearly magazine of educational resources and ideas for promoting respect for diversity, free to teachers.

U.S. Holocaust Memorial Council
2000 L Street NW, Suite 588
Washington, DC 20036
(202) 653-9220
Sponsors education projects.

The Women's International League for Peace and Freedom
1213 Race Street
Philadelphia, PA 19107-1691
(215) 563-7110
This international organization has local branches in U.S. cities, and publishes the news magazine *Peace and Freedom* six times a year.

Recommended Reading

Allport, Gordon. *The Nature of Prejudice.* Twenty-fifth anniversary edition. Reading, MA: Addison-Wesley Publishing Company, 1979.

Angelou, Maya. *Wouldn't Take Nothing for My Journey Now.* New York: Random House, 1993.

Baird, Robert M., and Stuart E. Rosenbaum, editors. *Bigotry, Prejudice and Hatred: Definitions, Causes and Solutions.* Buffalo: Prometheus Books, 1992.

Bateson, Mary Catherine. *Peripheral Visions: Learning Along the Way.* New York: HarperCollins, 1994.

Berry, Wendell. *The Hidden Wound.* San Francisco: North Point Press, 1989.

Bettner, Betty Lou, and Amy Lew. *Raising Kids Who Can: Using Family Meetings to Nurture Responsible, Cooperative, Caring, and Happy Children.* New York: HarperCollins, 1992.

Brown, Wesley, and Amy Ling, editors. *Imagining America: Stories from the Promised Land.* New York: Persea Books, 1991.

————*Visions of America: Personal Narratives from the Promised Land: A Multicultural Anthology of Autobiography and Essay.* New York: Persea Books, 1993.

Clark, Kenneth B. *Prejudice and Your Child.* Middletown, CT: Wesleyan University Press, 1963.

Cohen, Leah Hager. *Train Go Sorry: Inside a Deaf World.* Boston: Houghton Mifflin Company, 1994.

Coles, Robert. *The Moral Life of Children.* Boston: Atlantic Monthly Press, 1986.

————*The Spiritual Life of Children*. Boston: Houghton Mifflin Company, 1990.

Comer, James P., M.D., and Alvin F. Poussaint, M.D. *Raising Black Children*. New York: Plume, 1992.

Dalton, Harlon. *Racial Healing*. New York: Doubleday, 1995.

Derman-Sparks, Louise. *Anti-Bias Curriculum Tools for Empowering Young Children*. Washington, DC: The National Association for Education of Young Children, 1989.

Dew, Robb Forman. *The Family Heart: A Memoir of When Our Son Came Out*. Reading, MA: Addison-Wesley Publishing Company, 1994.

Edelman, Marian Wright. *The Measure of Our Success: A Letter to My Children and Yours*. Boston: Beacon Press, 1992.

Edward, Carolyn Pope, with Patricia Ramsey. *Promoting Social and Moral Development in Young Children: Creative Approaches for the Classroom*. New York: Teachers College Press, 1986.

Eisenberg, Nancy. *The Caring Child*. Cambridge, MA: Harvard University Press, 1992.

Eyre, Linda, and Richard. *Teaching Your Children Values*. New York: Simon & Schuster, 1993.

Faber, Adele, and Elaine Mazlish. *How to Talk So Kids Will Listen and Listen So Kids Will Talk*. New York: Avon Books, 1980. (The authors have also created a workshop kit for parenting groups. For more information, write to Workshop Kit; PO Box 64; Albertson, NY 11507)

Fitzpatrick, Jean Grasso. *Something More: Nurturing Your Child's Spiritual Growth*. New York: Penguin Books, 1991.

Hewlett, Sylvia Ann. *When the Bough Breaks: The Cost of Neglecting Our Children*. New York: HarperCollins, 1991.

Hopson, Dr. Darlene Powell, and Dr. Derek S. Hopson. *Different and Wonderful: Raising Black Children in a Race-Conscious Society*. New York: Fireside, 1990.

King, Martin Luther, Jr. *A Testament of Hope: The Essential Writings and Speeches of Martin Luther King, Jr.*, edited by James Melvin Washington. HarperSanFrancisco, 1986.

Konner, Melvin. *Childhood: A Multicultural View*. Boston: Little, Brown and Company, 1991.

Leach, Penelope. *Children First: What Our Society Must Do—And Is Not Doing—for Our Children Today.* New York: Alfred A. Knopf, 1994.

Louv, Richard. *Childhood's Future.* New York: Anchor Books, 1990.

————*101 Things You Can Do For Our Children's Future.* New York: Anchor Books, 1994.

Matiella, Ana Consuelo. *Positively Different: Creating a Bias-Free Environment for Young Children.* Santa Cruz, CA: Network Publications, 1991.

McGinnis, James, editor. *Helping Teens Care.* New York: Crossroad, 1991.

More, Thomas. *Care of the Soul: A Guide for Cultivating Depth and Sacredness in Everyday Life.* New York: HarperCollins, 1992.

Moses, Jeffrey. *Oneness: Great Principles Shared by All Religions.* New York: Fawcett Columbine, 1989.

Nelson, Jane. *Positive Discipline.* New York: Ballantine Books, 1987.

Nouwen, Henri J. M. *Reaching Out: The Three Movements of the Spiritual Life.* New York: Image Books, 1986.

Novak, Philip. *The World's Wisdom: Sacred Texts of the World's Religions.* HarperSanFrancisco, 1994.

Paley, Vivian. *You Can't Say You Can't Play.* Cambridge, MA: Harvard University Press, 1992.

Peck, M. Scott. *A World Waiting to Be Born: Civility Revisited.* New York: Bantam Books, 1993.

Riley, Sue Spayth. *How to Generate Values in Young Children.* Washington, DC: National Association for the Education of Young Children, 1984.

Schulman, Michael, and Eva Mekler. *Bringing Up a Moral Child: A New Approach for Teaching Your Child To be Kind, Just, and Responsible.* Reading, MA: Addison-Wesley Publishing Company, 1985.

Terkel, Studs. *Race: How Blacks and Whites Think and Feel About the American Obsession.* New York: The New Press, 1992.

Wilson, James Q. *The Moral Sense.* New York: The Free Press, 1993.

FAMILY RESOURCES

Multicultural Bibliographies

The first edition of *Kaleidoscope: A Multicultural Booklist for Grades K–8* annotates nearly four hundred books published between 1990 and 1992. Selections include fiction and nonfiction, grouped by theme, genre, and age level.

National Council of Teachers of English
1111 W. Kenyon Road
Urbana, IL 61801-1096
(217) 328-3870

Our Family, Our Friends, Our World: An Annotated Guide to Significant Multicultural Books for Children and Teenagers. A group of children's librarians selected a thousand of the best multicultural fiction and nonfiction books published between 1970 and 1990, categorized them according to age level and cultural origin, and provided detailed summaries of each recommended book, in the most complete bibliography of its type available.

R. R. Bowker Co.
121 Chanlon Road
New Providence, NJ 07974
(800) 521-8110

The African-American Experience: An HBJ Resource Guide for the Multicultural Classroom is an annotated bibliography of materials useful to parents interested in multicultural education and in African-American history and culture. The guide is divided into three sections. The first lists books on topics such as free blacks, the civil war, and the civil rights movement. The second lists resources for multicultural education. The final section lists fiction and nonfiction books appropriate for children.

Harcourt Brace Jovanovich
6277 Sea Harbor Drive
Orlando, FL 32887
(800) CALL-HBJ

The 474-page *Guide to Multicultural Resources* offers chapters on African, Asian Pacific, Hispanic, Native, and multicultural American organizations. Chapters are further subdivided into such categories as arts, civil rights, religious, and women's organizations. This is an extraordinarily thorough reference book—the most complete of its kind.

Highsmith Press
PO Box 800
Fort Atkinson, WI 53538
(800) 558-2110

Community Dialogue

Community leaders interested in solving racial and ethnic conflicts will find *Facing Racial and Cultural Conflict: Tools for Rebuilding Community* an easy-to-use manual. Profiling twenty-five successful collaborative efforts across the United States, the manual offers substantial guidance on how to create communities free of hate and intolerance.

Program for Community Problem Solving
915 15th Street, Suite 600
Washington, DC 20005

Can't We All Just Get Along? A Manual for Discussion Programs on Racism and Race Relations includes an introduction to the issue and suggests ways "study circles" can help address racism. The manual outlines five discussion sessions and provides recommendations for tailoring discussions to a particular community's concerns.

Study Circles Resource Center
PO Box 203
Pomfret, CT 06258
(203) 928-2616

Healing the Heart of America is a video and resource guide aimed at enabling community groups to begin "an honest conversation on race, reconciliation, and responsibility." The guide includes discussion starters, strategies for action, recommended reading, and a description of how the racial dialogue process worked to build bridges between blacks and whites in Richmond, VA.

Hope in the Cities
1103 Sunset Avenue
Richmond, VA 23221
(803) 358-1769

Children's Book Publishers

The Oryx Multicultural Folktale Series offers a variety of titles that explore surprising resemblances among the world's folktales. *Cinderella,* for example, not only tells the Cinderella story as we have come to know it but gives the "original" French medieval tale and recounts parallel stories from twenty-five other cultures, including Norwegian, ancient Egyptian, Iraqi, and Zuñi. Other titles include *A Knock at the Door, Beauties and the Beasts,* and *Tom Thumb.* (Grades 1–4)

The Oryx Press
4041 N. Central Avenue, Suite 700
Phoenix, AZ 85012
(800) 279-6799

Newbery Award–winning novels abound in the new LIFT series from Sundance, sets of four to six books that highlight topics such as the experiences of immigrants and minority groups. The teaching guides that accompany the books are unusually thorough and well organized and provide an abundance of ideas and activity suggestions. Many of the books, such as William Armstrong's *Sounder* and Betty Bao Lord's *In the Year of the Boar and Jackie Robinson,* are classics of children's literature. Other sets explore such themes as heroism, the natural world, and biography. (Grades 4–8)

Sundance Publishing
PO Box 1326
Littleton, MA 01460
(800) 343-8204

From *Aunt Harriet's Underground Railroad,* to Whoopi Goldberg's *Alice,* to *The Calypso Alphabet,* parents can find a wealth of African-American stories, poems, tales, and histories in the Books for Our Children catalog.

Books For Our Children
217 East 85 Street, Suite 184
New York, NY 10028
(212) 249-2743

Two series of texts for secondary students reinforce democratic values and coping skills. The *Values Library* series includes: *Cooperation; Tolerance; Self-Esteem; Citizenship;* and

Compassion. The *Coping With: Facing Challenges* series in-
cludes *Coping with Bias Incidents; Coping with Verbal Abuse;
Coping with Discrimination; Coping with Cross-Cultural and
Interracial Relationships; Coping with Your Sexual Orientation;* and *Coping with a Bigoted Parent.* Videos for teenagers
include: *Acting on Your Values; Communicating with Parents;
Racism;* and *High Five: Celebrating African-American Teens.*
Multicultural books include *The Heritage Library of African
Peoples;* fifty-six books focusing on African cultures; and *Ica-
rus,* a collection of global literature; *In Their Own Voices,* oral
histories of teenage refugees; and *The Library of Social Activ-
ism,* which includes books for teenagers on combating hate
groups, world hunger, homelessness, and human rights violations.

The Rosen Publishing Group
29 East 21 Street
New York, NY 10010
(800) 237-9932

Elementary school students wrote and illustrated a series of
books introducing other children to various cultures and to
the lives of children with special needs. *Becoming Myself* includes true stories about growing up African American and
helps lead teenagers toward greater self-esteem. Other titles
for children and teenagers promote self-esteem and multicultural understanding through meditations, humor, creative activities, and board games.

Free Spirit Publishing
400 First Avenue N, Suite 616
Minneapolis, MN 55401-1730
(800) 735-7323

A wide range of culturally diverse children's literature with an emphasis on Asian studies are supplemented by a translation service and a children's multicultural book club at Shen's Books.

Shen's Books and Supplies
821 S. First Avenue
Arcadia, CA 91006
(800) 456-6660

Claudia Temple, whose adopted children were born outside the United States, made a business of finding multicultural resources for her children. In her effort to bring other cultures into her home, she discovered a range of books, toys, and other educational items that she now offers through catalogue sales.

Colors of Harmony
5767 Foser Road
Bainbridge Island, WA 98110
(800) 283-5659

The series *Lives of Notable Gay Men and Lesbians* features books on Willa Cather, John Maynard Keynes, Gertrude Stein, and Harvey Milk among its thirty or so titles. Its biography of James Baldwin is an elegantly thoughtful examination of Baldwin's complicated and sometimes prickly character. (Grades 10 and up)

Chelsea House Publishers
300 Park Avenue South
New York, NY 10010
(800) 848-BOOK

As its name signifies, Polychrome Publishing Corporation celebrates the full spectrum of our human community. Since 1990 this Chicago children's press has been producing imaginative, visually appealing books that promote respect for racial, ethnic, cultural, and religious differences. The stories often reflect the personal experiences of the authors, who represent many heritages. Among their titles for grades 4–7: *Ashok By Any Other Name; Char Siu Bao Boy;* and *Almond Cookies and Dragon Well Tea.* Polychrome donates a portion of its proceeds to other projects pursuing similar ideals.

Polychrome
Publishing Corp.
4509 N. Francisco Avenue
Chicago, IL 60625-3808
(312) 478-0786

Lee and Low Books specializes in multicultural literature for young readers, including: *Bein' With You This Way,* a playground rap between an African American and a group of her friends who discover their differences and similarities; *Amelia's Road,* the story of a young girl from a migrant worker family who finally finds a place of belonging; and *Baseball Saved Us,* an award-winning book about a young Japanese American whose love for baseball helped him endure life in an internment camp.

Lee and Low Books
228 East 45 Street
New York, NY 10017
(212) 867-6155

Immigration is given a searching and balanced treatment in two handbooks published by the New Faces of Liberty Project. The handbooks explore the reasons for recent immigration from Central America, the Caribbean, and Southeast Asia and introduce students to the history of these regions and America's ambivalent attitudes toward refugees. They also provide activity suggestions to encourage students to find solutions to the stereotyping and violence that can result when immigrants move into a neighborhood school. The reality of the immigrant experience is brought to life in these handbooks with oral histories from immigrant children themselves. *New Faces of Liberty* and *New Faces in Our Schools* are for grades 5–12.

Many Cultures Publishing
1095 Market Street, Suite 602
San Francisco, CA 94103
(800) 484-4173, ext. 1073

Bilingual, multicultural books for children are the specialty of Children's Book Press. Titles include a folktale of the Hmong people, a Native American story, a Miskito Indian legend, an adaptation of a Mexican poem, and many more. Each book is told and illustrated by people from the same ethnic group highlighted in the story.

Children's Book Press
6400 Hollis Street, Suite 4
Emeryville, CA 94608
(510) 655-3395

Illustrated rhyming books for young children about various cultures and easy-to-read biographies of notable Americans of various ethnic backgrounds are included in the multicultural offerings of Childrens Press.

Childrens Press
5440 N. Cumberland Ave.
Chicago, IL 60656-1494
(800) 621-1115

Founded in 1980, the National Women's History Project is dedicated to promoting a deeper understanding of women's roles in American history and society. It produces a large number of videos, books, posters, newsletters, and curriculum materials, and through its Women's History Catalog gives teachers access to these and hundreds of other items of related interest. The Multicultural Women's History Curriculum Unit offers biographies of five women of unusual compassion, courage, and conviction. The unit is one in a series for children in K–6 that highlights such extraordinary women as Abigail Adams, Mary McLeod Bethune, and Helen Keller.

National Women's History Project
7738 Bell Road, Dept. P
Windsor, CA 95492
(707) 838-6000

Tired of the cynical commercial vision of American girlhood? Twenty young women in Duluth, Minnesota, ages eight to fourteen, have come up with a refreshing alternative. *New Moon* is a bimonthly magazine of news, views, health tips, activities, and enlightening ideas, mostly contributed and edited by girls. The sharp-looking publication is chockfull of positive role models, stories from world cultures, and the lively voices of girls rising to their full potential. The same group of girls and their parents also publish the bimonthly *New Moon Parenting*.

New Moon
PO Box 3587
Duluth, MN 55803
(218) 728-5507

Dedicated to the publication of children's and young adult literature by Hispanic authors, Piñata Books offers books that portray themes, characters, and customs unique to the American Hispanic experience.

Piñata Books
Arte Público Press
University of Houston
Houston, TX 77204-2090
(800) 633-ARTE

The *Jewish Kids Catalog* is the ultimate treasure house of things Jewish for children ages eight and above. From home life to history to Jewish culture around the world, the book offers enough interesting facts, pictures, and activity ideas to satisfy the most curious young minds. And when they're ready for more, there's an excellent bibliography.

Jewish Publication Society
1930 Chestnut Street
Philadelphia, PA 19103
(800) 355-1165

The novels, biographies, and books for young children published by Just Us all focus on positive images of African American life. A bimonthly newspaper called *Harambee* introduces young readers to topics related to the African American experience.

Just Us Books, Inc.
301 Main Street
Orange, NJ 07050
(201) 672-7701

In *Class of 2000: The Prejudice Puzzle,* National Public Radio examines the effects of prejudice on young people today by interviewing several of its victims, including a high school champion athlete who happens to be a dwarf, an academically gifted black teenager whose aggressive manner caused him to be barred from public school, and children at a "fat camp" in the Catskills. The effect of the three-cassette package is surprisingly powerful. Because we can't see the people being interviewed, the external conditions that provoke discrimination seem particularly irrelevant. Teaching guide included. (Grades 6 and up)

National Public Radio Outreach
635 Massachusetts Avenue N.W.
Washington, DC 20001
(202) 414-2843

Other multicultural publishers include: Positive Images (Brooklyn, NY); Lift Every Voice (Newton Centre, MA); Open Hand Books, Parenting Press, Morning Glory, Blue Heron, Bright Ring. For information on these and other multicultural publishers, contact:

Friends of the CCBC
(Cooperative Children's Book Center)
Box 5288
Madison, WI 53705-0288
or
Multicultural Publishers Exchange
PO Box 9869
Madison, WI 53715

Dolls, Toys, Art, and Games

Magnetic Hebrew letters, African percussion instruments, Asian and Hispanic play foods, and dolls with handicaps are among the wonderful assortment of multicultural fun stuff from Constructive Playthings. You'll also find books, music, puzzles, and dolls of every color.

Constructive Playthings
1227 E. 199th Street
Grandview, MO 64030-1117
(800) 448-4115

People of the World is an eight-foot-long poster crammed with facts and illustrations exhibiting human diversity. The single most extraordinary poster we've seen, it is bursting with vivid, detailed portraits of the world's peoples and life styles. From the book of the same name.

Anatomical Chart Co.
8221 Kimball Avenue
Skokie, IL 60076
(800) 621-7500

The Ancient and Living Cultures Series is a set of ten stencil books featuring tales, myths, and art projects derived from different cultures, including the Yoruba of West Africa, the Indians of the Southwest, and the ancient Japanese. The punch-out stencils give children an entry into the cultures, and the projects, which include making a samurai helmet, a ceremonial headdress, a totem pole, and a model pyramid, are imaginative and fun. The introduction to each book provides easy-to-understand background information on the beliefs and traditions of the culture. (Grades 3 and up)

Good Year Books
1900 E. Lake Avenue
Glenview, IL 60025
(800) 628-4480, ext. 3038

Remember the color in the old crayon box marked FLESH? Did it ever really match anybody's skin? Creative colorists can now choose from a rainbow of warm shades in *People Colors,* a collection of crayons, tempera paints, markers, and craft paper. The crayons come in two sizes and twenty-four tones, while the other media offer twelve colors. Call for prices.

Lakeshore Learning Materials
PO Box 6261
Carson, CA 90749
(800) 421-5354

Cynthia's Toys carries over two hundred multicultural books, videos, and cassettes, as well as strikingly beautiful dolls of different ethnicities and races, from infancy to adult-hood. African musical instruments, an African map puzzle, and math game are also available.

Cynthia's Toys
501 14th Street
City Center Square
Oakland, CA 94612
(510) 464-3646

To give children a sense of the diversity of the real world, teachers are beginning to use "personal dolls"—dolls that have their own personalities, family makeups, ethnic origins, and abilities. The dolls offered by People of Every Stripe are characterized by their uniqueness. They have different facial features, hair texture, and skin color. There's a balding older man, a Down syndrome boy, a girl with a prosthetic leg, and a blind boy with a cane.

> People of Every Stripe
> PO Box 12505
> Portland, OR 97212
> (503) 282-0612

Let's Play Chinese Games is a children's book and a comprehensive teacher's guide. English and Chinese texts describe the making and playing of three traditional Chinese children's games: Yin, rubber-band jump rope, and Chinese jacks. Worksheets show children how to write Chinese characters.

> Institute for Intercultural Studies
> 11729 Gateway Boulevard
> Los Angeles, CA 90064
> (310) 479-6045

Keisha Doll Company offers more than forty dolls in a variety of skin tones and dress styles (including traditional African dress), as well as dolls that represent historical figures.

> Keisha Doll Company
> 524 West 174 Street
> New York, NY 10033

Music

MULTICULTURAL FUN

We All Sing Together is a Sesame Street Home Videos spectacular starring Herry the anchormonster. In an investigative news show format, Herry discovers that kids, like all of us (monsters included!), can be different in some ways and the same in others. Nine jazzy songs illustrate how kids can have different hair styles, skin colors, and family structures, yet share a common humanity. Complete with song-lyric poster. (Grades K–4)

Random House Home Video
201 East 50 Street
New York, NY 10022
(800) 733-3000

World Music Press offers music and social studies teachers a worldwide selection of books and recordings. These book-cassette kits are recommended for all age groups: *Let Your Voice Be Heard: Songs From Ghana and Zimbabwe; Silent Temples, Songful Hearts: Traditional Music of Cambodia;* and *From Rice Paddies and Temple Yards: Traditional Music of Vietnam.* Accompanying books include maps, pictures, study guides, and glossaries, and note relevant historical, musical, and cultural information.

World Music Press
PO Box 2565
Danbury, CT 06813-2565
(203) 748-1131

Joining Hands with Other Lands helps young children to explore world cultures through music. The sixteen songs come with lyrics and suggested games and activities.

Kimbo Educational
PO Box 477
10 N. Third Avenue
Long Branch, NJ 07740
(800) 631-2187

Under One Sky encourages children to sing along to songs with visions of a caring world. *As Strong As Anyone Can Be* is loaded with songs promoting positive self-images for girls.

A Gentle Wind
PO Box 3103
Albany, NY 12203-0103
(518) 436-0391

Caribbean Carnival: Songs of the West Indies contains music, words, and chord symbols for thirteen songs, such as "Jamaica Farewell," "Yellow Bird," and "Day-O." Each song is accompanied by a brilliant painting depicting life in the Caribbean.

William Morrow & Co.
1350 Avenue of the Americas
New York, NY 10019
(800) 843-9389

In *Reggae For Kids,* twelve influential reggae musicians, including Gregory Isaacs, Yellowman, and Bunny Wailer, sing favorite songs with joyful enthusiasm and irresistible rhythm. A wide range of music and musical instruments from various cultures is included in this catalogue of resources for children.

Music for Little People
PO Box 1460
Redway, CA 95560
(800) 727-2233

Best of Ladysmith Black Mambazo presents harmonic pleasures from black South Africa for the entire family. Sweet Honey in the Rock's *In This Land* and *Live at Carnegie Hall* capture the rich congregational tradition of African American music.

Music for Little People
PO Box 1460
Redway, CA 95560
(800) 727-2233

Three of Dr. Martin Luther King's speeches, *I've Been to the Mountain, I Have a Dream,* and *The Drum Major Instinct,* are available on cassette. Ella Jenkins offers children a journey through several cultures in song, including call and response songs using a children's choir. Black history playing cards, coloring books, and posters are also available.

Claudia's Caravan
Multicultural/Multilingual Materials
PO Box 1582
Alameda, CA 94501
(415) 521-7871

Children's Stories

The theme of diversity shines in three beautifully illustrated children's books. *The Keys to My Kingdom* takes the classic Mother Goose poem and presents it in English, French, and Spanish. *Dragon Kite of the Autumn Moon* connects a yearly Taiwanese tradition with a young boy's attempt to heal his grandfather. *Mandy,* the story of a young deaf child, was written by a teacher for the deaf.

Lothrop, Lee and Shepard Books
39 Plymouth Street
Fairfield, NJ 07007
(800) 843-9389

Both a testament of enduring maternal love and an introduction to historic Inuit life, *Mama, Do You Love Me?* is a lyrical picture book. A small child questions the limits of her mother's love, and her mother's archetypal answers are accompanied by rich Inuit symbols and culture. A glossary of Inuit terms is included.

Chronicle Books
275 Fifth Street
San Francisco, CA 94103
(800) 722-6657

Amazing Grace gives young children a model of independence in a young girl who believes she can be anything she wants to be. When she tries out for the role of Peter Pan in the school play, two classmates object because she is black and a girl. With the encouragement of her mother and grandmother, Grace persists.

Dial Books for Young Readers
Penguin USA
120 Woodbine Street
Bergenfield, NJ 07621
(800) 253-6476

Gwen Everett's *Li'l Sis and Uncle Willie*, although fiction, captures the emotional bond between a sensitive, famous uncle and his beloved niece. Based on the life of the African American artist William Johnson, and illustrated with his paintings, *Li'l Sis and Uncle Willie* also chronicles a child's growing understanding of racism and pride.

Rizzoli
300 Park Avenue South
New York, NY 10010
(212) 387-3400

Stereotypes are scrutinized in three children's books. In *You Be Me, I'll Be You* (Belgium), a white father convinces his biracial daughter that she is perfect the way she is. In *Tusk Tusk* (England), white and black elephants seek to destroy each other. In *Paul and Sebastian*, parents refuse to allow their sons to play together because one lives in an apartment and the other in a trailer. *The Night of the Stars* is a beautifully illustrated South American legend.

Kane/Miller Book Publishers
PO Box 8515
La Jolla, CA 92038-8515
(619) 456-0540

Families Are Different and *The Fourth Question: A Chinese Tale* are two beautifully illustrated books for young children. *Families Are Different* is a story about an adopted Korean girl who learns that it's OK to be adopted because love makes every family special. *The Fourth Question* is a Chinese tale about a poor farmer who learns that doing good deeds brings happiness and rewards.

Holiday House
425 Madison Avenue
New York, NY 10017
(212) 688-0085

Abuela is a beautiful children's book about a little girl, her grandmother, and their colorful and imaginative trip through New York City. The story is told in English spiced with Spanish phrases. The book includes a glossary of Spanish terms. *The Tale of the Mandarin Ducks* is a popular Japanese folktale that elementary school children will enjoy. Brilliant watercolor and pastel illustrations accompany this engaging story.

Penguin USA
375 Hudson Street
New York, NY 10014-3657
(800) 526-0275

Teammates is a story about Jackie Robinson's first baseball season with the Brooklyn Dodgers and the hardships he endured as the first black man to play on a major league baseball team. Those hardships were lessened during a game with the Cincinnati Reds, when his Southern-born teammate Pee Wee Reese publicly declared his support for Robinson. Appropriate for elementary grades, this book is loaded with dramatic watercolor paintings and rare baseball photographs.

Harcourt Brace Jovanovich
6277 Sea Harbor Drive
Orlando, FL 32821
(800) CALL-HBJ

A Letter to the King by Leong Va' is a story about bravery in the ancient Chinese empire. When all else fails, Ti Ying, the youngest daughter of a doctor, courageously rescues her father from prison and delivers a plea to the king to pardon her father.

Harper Collins Publishers
1000 Keystone Industrial Park
Scranton, PA 18512
(800) 242-7737

Thirteen Moons on Turtle's Back: A Native American Year of Moons explores Native American culture through stories and poems about the thirteen moons of the year. Young children will find the book's oil paintings exciting and realistic. *Northern Lullaby* uses Native American characters and the calm Alaska winter's landscape to offer a warm and perfect bedtime lullaby.

The Putnam and Grosset Group
200 Madison Avenue
New York, NY 10016
(800) 847-5515
In NY: (607) 775-1740

In *Father Gander's Nursery Rhymes: The Equal Rhymes Amendment,* Dr. Doug Larche has rewritten traditional Mother Goose nursery rhymes to reinforce the values of equality, love, and responsibility. "Mr. and Ms. Pumpkin Eater," for example:

> Peter, Peter, pumpkin eater
> Had a wife and wished to keep her
> Treated her with fair respect,
> She stayed with him
> and hugged his neck!

Advocacy Press
PO Box 236
Santa Barbara, CA 93102
(805) 962-2728

The Girl Who Loved Caterpillars retells a story discovered on a twelfth-century Japanese scroll and creates a vivid portrait of a free-spirited girl who is determined to be herself. Young women will find the main character, Izumi, inspiring, as she refuses to give in to her society's strict notions of women's roles.

The Putnam and Grosset Group
200 Madison Avenue
New York, NY 10016
(800) 847-5515

Resources
for Social Action

The Directory of American Youth Organizations is written for young people who want to become involved in community-building activities through a wide range of organizations. *Respecting Our Differences: A Guide to Getting Along in a Changing World* helps young people (ages thirteen and up) to understand the nature of prejudice and the rewards of tolerance.

Free Spirit Publishing
400 First Avenue
Minneapolis, MN 55401
(612) 338-2068

50 Ways to Help Your Community includes stories of adults and children who have found innovative ways to improve their communities, as well as information for contacting a variety of organizations.

Doubleday
1540 Broadway
New York, NY 10036

Jimmy Carter's *Talking Peace: A Vision for the Next Generation* offers a characteristically thoughtful and generous view of the problems and promises of our new world order. The former president begins with a glance back at one of the highlights of his administration, the Camp David peace accords, which brought Israel and Egypt together. In the chapters that follow, he discusses human rights, the environment, the nature of peace and war, democratization, and our inner cities. Carter concludes by addressing the question of what young people can do to make the world a better place. (Grades 8–12)

Dutton Children's Books
375 Hudson Street
New York, NY 10014
(800) 526-0275

Index

225

About the Author

Sara Bullard, a graduate of the University of North Carolina, has worked for the past decade as a writer and editor in the field of human rights. She is the author of *Free at Last: A History of the Civil Rights Movement and Those Who Died in the Struggle,* and the director of the Teaching Tolerance project of the Southern Poverty Law Center in Montgomery, Alabama.